C-3176  CAREER EXAMINATION SERIES

*This is your*
*PASSBOOK for...*

# Supervising Public Health Adviser

*Test Preparation Study Guide*
*Questions & Answers*

# COPYRIGHT NOTICE

This book is SOLELY intended for, is sold ONLY to, and its use is RESTRICTED to individual, bona fide applicants or candidates who qualify by virtue of having seriously filed applications for appropriate license, certificate, professional and/or promotional advancement, higher school matriculation, scholarship, or other legitimate requirements of education and/or governmental authorities.

This book is NOT intended for use, class instruction, tutoring, training, duplication, copying, reprinting, excerption, or adaptation, etc., by:

1) Other publishers
2) Proprietors and/or Instructors of "Coaching" and/or Preparatory Courses
3) Personnel and/or Training Divisions of commercial, industrial, and governmental organizations
4) Schools, colleges, or universities and/or their departments and staffs, including teachers and other personnel
5) Testing Agencies or Bureaus
6) Study groups which seek by the purchase of a single volume to copy and/or duplicate and/or adapt this material for use by the group as a whole without having purchased individual volumes for each of the members of the group
7) Et al.

Such persons would be in violation of appropriate Federal and State statutes.

PROVISION OF LICENSING AGREEMENTS – Recognized educational, commercial, industrial, and governmental institutions and organizations, and others legitimately engaged in educational pursuits, including training, testing, and measurement activities, may address request for a licensing agreement to the copyright owners, who will determine whether, and under what conditions, including fees and charges, the materials in this book may be used them. In other words, a licensing facility exists for the legitimate use of the material in this book on other than an individual basis. However, it is asseverated and affirmed here that the material in this book CANNOT be used without the receipt of the express permission of such a licensing agreement from the Publishers. Inquiries re licensing should be addressed to the company, attention rights and permissions department.

All rights reserved, including the right of reproduction in whole or in part, in any form or by any means, electronic or mechanical, including photocopying, recording, or by any information storage and retrieval system, without permission in writing from the Publisher.

Copyright © 2024 by
## National Learning Corporation

212 Michael Drive, Syosset, NY 11791
(516) 921-8888 • www.passbooks.com
E-mail: info@passbooks.com

# PASSBOOK® SERIES

THE *PASSBOOK® SERIES* has been created to prepare applicants and candidates for the ultimate academic battlefield – the examination room.

At some time in our lives, each and every one of us may be required to take an examination – for validation, matriculation, admission, qualification, registration, certification, or licensure.

Based on the assumption that every applicant or candidate has met the basic formal educational standards, has taken the required number of courses, and read the necessary texts, the *PASSBOOK® SERIES* furnishes the one special preparation which may assure passing with confidence, instead of failing with insecurity. Examination questions – together with answers – are furnished as the basic vehicle for study so that the mysteries of the examination and its compounding difficulties may be eliminated or diminished by a sure method.

This book is meant to help you pass your examination provided that you qualify and are serious in your objective.

The entire field is reviewed through the huge store of content information which is succinctly presented through a provocative and challenging approach – the question-and-answer method.

A climate of success is established by furnishing the correct answers at the end of each test.

You soon learn to recognize types of questions, forms of questions, and patterns of questioning. You may even begin to anticipate expected outcomes.

You perceive that many questions are repeated or adapted so that you can gain acute insights, which may enable you to score many sure points.

You learn how to confront new questions, or types of questions, and to attack them confidently and work out the correct answers.

You note objectives and emphases, and recognize pitfalls and dangers, so that you may make positive educational adjustments.

Moreover, you are kept fully informed in relation to new concepts, methods, practices, and directions in the field.

You discover that you are actually taking the examination all the time: you are preparing for the examination by "taking" an examination, not by reading extraneous and/or supererogatory textbooks.

In short, this PASSBOOK®, used directedly, should be an important factor in helping you to pass your test.

# SUPERVISING PUBLIC HEALTH ADVISER

DUTIES AND RESPONSIBILITIES
Supervises staff personnel in the planning, organizing, and conducting of communicable disease control efforts. Areas of concern are epidemiological activities; hospital, laboratory and physician surveillance and liaison; and lay and professional education. Performs related work.

SCOPE OF THE EXAMINATION
The written test may include questions concerning communicable disease control, public health, and human behavior; interviewing and investigation techniques; preparing and understanding statistical charts; supervision; and other related areas.

# HOW TO TAKE A TEST

I. YOU MUST PASS AN EXAMINATION

*A. WHAT EVERY CANDIDATE SHOULD KNOW*

Examination applicants often ask us for help in preparing for the written test. What can I study in advance? What kinds of questions will be asked? How will the test be given? How will the papers be graded?

As an applicant for a civil service examination, you may be wondering about some of these things. Our purpose here is to suggest effective methods of advance study and to describe civil service examinations.

Your chances for success on this examination can be increased if you know how to prepare. Those "pre-examination jitters" can be reduced if you know what to expect. You can even experience an adventure in good citizenship if you know why civil service exams are given.

*B. WHY ARE CIVIL SERVICE EXAMINATIONS GIVEN?*

Civil service examinations are important to you in two ways. As a citizen, you want public jobs filled by employees who know how to do their work. As a job seeker, you want a fair chance to compete for that job on an equal footing with other candidates. The best-known means of accomplishing this two-fold goal is the competitive examination.

Exams are widely publicized throughout the nation. They may be administered for jobs in federal, state, city, municipal, town or village governments or agencies.

Any citizen may apply, with some limitations, such as the age or residence of applicants. Your experience and education may be reviewed to see whether you meet the requirements for the particular examination. When these requirements exist, they are reasonable and applied consistently to all applicants. Thus, a competitive examination may cause you some uneasiness now, but it is your privilege and safeguard.

*C. HOW ARE CIVIL SERVICE EXAMS DEVELOPED?*

Examinations are carefully written by trained technicians who are specialists in the field known as "psychological measurement," in consultation with recognized authorities in the field of work that the test will cover. These experts recommend the subject matter areas or skills to be tested; only those knowledges or skills important to your success on the job are included. The most reliable books and source materials available are used as references. Together, the experts and technicians judge the difficulty level of the questions.

Test technicians know how to phrase questions so that the problem is clearly stated. Their ethics do not permit "trick" or "catch" questions. Questions may have been tried out on sample groups, or subjected to statistical analysis, to determine their usefulness.

Written tests are often used in combination with performance tests, ratings of training and experience, and oral interviews. All of these measures combine to form the best-known means of finding the right person for the right job.

## II. HOW TO PASS THE WRITTEN TEST

### A. NATURE OF THE EXAMINATION

To prepare intelligently for civil service examinations, you should know how they differ from school examinations you have taken. In school you were assigned certain definite pages to read or subjects to cover. The examination questions were quite detailed and usually emphasized memory. Civil service exams, on the other hand, try to discover your present ability to perform the duties of a position, plus your potentiality to learn these duties. In other words, a civil service exam attempts to predict how successful you will be. Questions cover such a broad area that they cannot be as minute and detailed as school exam questions.

In the public service similar kinds of work, or positions, are grouped together in one "class." This process is known as *position-classification*. All the positions in a class are paid according to the salary range for that class. One class title covers all of these positions, and they are all tested by the same examination.

### B. FOUR BASIC STEPS

#### 1) Study the announcement

How, then, can you know what subjects to study? Our best answer is: "Learn as much as possible about the class of positions for which you've applied." The exam will test the knowledge, skills and abilities needed to do the work.

Your most valuable source of information about the position you want is the official exam announcement. This announcement lists the training and experience qualifications. Check these standards and apply only if you come reasonably close to meeting them.

The brief description of the position in the examination announcement offers some clues to the subjects which will be tested. Think about the job itself. Review the duties in your mind. Can you perform them, or are there some in which you are rusty? Fill in the blank spots in your preparation.

Many jurisdictions preview the written test in the exam announcement by including a section called "Knowledge and Abilities Required," "Scope of the Examination," or some similar heading. Here you will find out specifically what fields will be tested.

#### 2) Review your own background

Once you learn in general what the position is all about, and what you need to know to do the work, ask yourself which subjects you already know fairly well and which need improvement. You may wonder whether to concentrate on improving your strong areas or on building some background in your fields of weakness. When the announcement has specified "some knowledge" or "considerable knowledge," or has used adjectives like "beginning principles of…" or "advanced … methods," you can get a clue as to the number and difficulty of questions to be asked in any given field. More questions, and hence broader coverage, would be included for those subjects which are more important in the work. Now weigh your strengths and weaknesses against the job requirements and prepare accordingly.

#### 3) Determine the level of the position

Another way to tell how intensively you should prepare is to understand the level of the job for which you are applying. Is it the entering level? In other words, is this the position in which beginners in a field of work are hired? Or is it an intermediate or advanced level? Sometimes this is indicated by such words as "Junior" or "Senior" in the class title. Other jurisdictions use Roman numerals to designate the level – Clerk I, Clerk II, for example. The word "Supervisor" sometimes appears in the title. If the level is not indicated by the title, check the description of duties. Will you be working under very close supervision, or will you have responsibility for independent decisions in this work?

### 4) Choose appropriate study materials

Now that you know the subjects to be examined and the relative amount of each subject to be covered, you can choose suitable study materials. For beginning level jobs, or even advanced ones, if you have a pronounced weakness in some aspect of your training, read a modern, standard textbook in that field. Be sure it is up to date and has general coverage. Such books are normally available at your library, and the librarian will be glad to help you locate one. For entry-level positions, questions of appropriate difficulty are chosen – neither highly advanced questions, nor those too simple. Such questions require careful thought but not advanced training.

If the position for which you are applying is technical or advanced, you will read more advanced, specialized material. If you are already familiar with the basic principles of your field, elementary textbooks would waste your time. Concentrate on advanced textbooks and technical periodicals. Think through the concepts and review difficult problems in your field.

These are all general sources. You can get more ideas on your own initiative, following these leads. For example, training manuals and publications of the government agency which employs workers in your field can be useful, particularly for technical and professional positions. A letter or visit to the government department involved may result in more specific study suggestions, and certainly will provide you with a more definite idea of the exact nature of the position you are seeking.

## III. KINDS OF TESTS

Tests are used for purposes other than measuring knowledge and ability to perform specified duties. For some positions, it is equally important to test ability to make adjustments to new situations or to profit from training. In others, basic mental abilities not dependent on information are essential. Questions which test these things may not appear as pertinent to the duties of the position as those which test for knowledge and information. Yet they are often highly important parts of a fair examination. For very general questions, it is almost impossible to help you direct your study efforts. What we can do is to point out some of the more common of these general abilities needed in public service positions and describe some typical questions.

1) General information

Broad, general information has been found useful for predicting job success in some kinds of work. This is tested in a variety of ways, from vocabulary lists to questions about current events. Basic background in some field of work, such as sociology or economics, may be sampled in a group of questions. Often these are principles which have become familiar to most persons through exposure rather than through formal training. It is difficult to advise you how to study for these questions; being alert to the world around you is our best suggestion.

2) Verbal ability

An example of an ability needed in many positions is verbal or language ability. Verbal ability is, in brief, the ability to use and understand words. Vocabulary and grammar tests are typical measures of this ability. Reading comprehension or paragraph interpretation questions are common in many kinds of civil service tests. You are given a paragraph of written material and asked to find its central meaning.

### 3) Numerical ability

Number skills can be tested by the familiar arithmetic problem, by checking paired lists of numbers to see which are alike and which are different, or by interpreting charts and graphs. In the latter test, a graph may be printed in the test booklet which you are asked to use as the basis for answering questions.

### 4) Observation

A popular test for law-enforcement positions is the observation test. A picture is shown to you for several minutes, then taken away. Questions about the picture test your ability to observe both details and larger elements.

### 5) Following directions

In many positions in the public service, the employee must be able to carry out written instructions dependably and accurately. You may be given a chart with several columns, each column listing a variety of information. The questions require you to carry out directions involving the information given in the chart.

### 6) Skills and aptitudes

Performance tests effectively measure some manual skills and aptitudes. When the skill is one in which you are trained, such as typing or shorthand, you can practice. These tests are often very much like those given in business school or high school courses. For many of the other skills and aptitudes, however, no short-time preparation can be made. Skills and abilities natural to you or that you have developed throughout your lifetime are being tested.

Many of the general questions just described provide all the data needed to answer the questions and ask you to use your reasoning ability to find the answers. Your best preparation for these tests, as well as for tests of facts and ideas, is to be at your physical and mental best. You, no doubt, have your own methods of getting into an exam-taking mood and keeping "in shape." The next section lists some ideas on this subject.

## IV. KINDS OF QUESTIONS

Only rarely is the "essay" question, which you answer in narrative form, used in civil service tests. Civil service tests are usually of the short-answer type. Full instructions for answering these questions will be given to you at the examination. But in case this is your first experience with short-answer questions and separate answer sheets, here is what you need to know:

### 1) Multiple-choice Questions

Most popular of the short-answer questions is the "multiple choice" or "best answer" question. It can be used, for example, to test for factual knowledge, ability to solve problems or judgment in meeting situations found at work.

A multiple-choice question is normally one of three types—

- It can begin with an incomplete statement followed by several possible endings. You are to find the one ending which *best* completes the statement, although some of the others may not be entirely wrong.
- It can also be a complete statement in the form of a question which is answered by choosing one of the statements listed.

- It can be in the form of a problem – again you select the best answer.

Here is an example of a multiple-choice question with a discussion which should give you some clues as to the method for choosing the right answer:

When an employee has a complaint about his assignment, the action which will *best* help him overcome his difficulty is to
   A. discuss his difficulty with his coworkers
   B. take the problem to the head of the organization
   C. take the problem to the person who gave him the assignment
   D. say nothing to anyone about his complaint

In answering this question, you should study each of the choices to find which is best. Consider choice "A" – Certainly an employee may discuss his complaint with fellow employees, but no change or improvement can result, and the complaint remains unresolved. Choice "B" is a poor choice since the head of the organization probably does not know what assignment you have been given, and taking your problem to him is known as "going over the head" of the supervisor. The supervisor, or person who made the assignment, is the person who can clarify it or correct any injustice. Choice "C" is, therefore, correct. To say nothing, as in choice "D," is unwise. Supervisors have and interest in knowing the problems employees are facing, and the employee is seeking a solution to his problem.

## 2) True/False Questions

The "true/false" or "right/wrong" form of question is sometimes used. Here a complete statement is given. Your job is to decide whether the statement is right or wrong.

SAMPLE: A roaming cell-phone call to a nearby city costs less than a non-roaming call to a distant city.

This statement is wrong, or false, since roaming calls are more expensive.
This is not a complete list of all possible question forms, although most of the others are variations of these common types. You will always get complete directions for answering questions. Be sure you understand *how* to mark your answers – ask questions until you do.

## V. RECORDING YOUR ANSWERS

Computer terminals are used more and more today for many different kinds of exams.
For an examination with very few applicants, you may be told to record your answers in the test booklet itself. Separate answer sheets are much more common. If this separate answer sheet is to be scored by machine – and this is often the case – it is highly important that you mark your answers correctly in order to get credit.
An electronic scoring machine is often used in civil service offices because of the speed with which papers can be scored. Machine-scored answer sheets must be marked with a pencil, which will be given to you. This pencil has a high graphite content which responds to the electronic scoring machine. As a matter of fact, stray dots may register as answers, so do not let your pencil rest on the answer sheet while you are pondering the correct answer. Also, if your pencil lead breaks or is otherwise defective, ask for another.

Since the answer sheet will be dropped in a slot in the scoring machine, be careful not to bend the corners or get the paper crumpled.

The answer sheet normally has five vertical columns of numbers, with 30 numbers to a column. These numbers correspond to the question numbers in your test booklet. After each number, going across the page are four or five pairs of dotted lines. These short dotted lines have small letters or numbers above them. The first two pairs may also have a "T" or "F" above the letters. This indicates that the first two pairs only are to be used if the questions are of the true-false type. If the questions are multiple choice, disregard the "T" and "F" and pay attention only to the small letters or numbers.

Answer your questions in the manner of the sample that follows:

32. The largest city in the United States is
    A. Washington, D.C.
    B. New York City
    C. Chicago
    D. Detroit
    E. San Francisco

1) Choose the answer you think is best. (New York City is the largest, so "B" is correct.)
2) Find the row of dotted lines numbered the same as the question you are answering. (Find row number 32)
3) Find the pair of dotted lines corresponding to the answer. (Find the pair of lines under the mark "B.")
4) Make a solid black mark between the dotted lines.


## VI. BEFORE THE TEST

Common sense will help you find procedures to follow to get ready for an examination. Too many of us, however, overlook these sensible measures. Indeed, nervousness and fatigue have been found to be the most serious reasons why applicants fail to do their best on civil service tests. Here is a list of reminders:

- Begin your preparation early – Don't wait until the last minute to go scurrying around for books and materials or to find out what the position is all about.
- Prepare continuously – An hour a night for a week is better than an all-night cram session. This has been definitely established. What is more, a night a week for a month will return better dividends than crowding your study into a shorter period of time.
- Locate the place of the exam – You have been sent a notice telling you when and where to report for the examination. If the location is in a different town or otherwise unfamiliar to you, it would be well to inquire the best route and learn something about the building.
- Relax the night before the test – Allow your mind to rest. Do not study at all that night. Plan some mild recreation or diversion; then go to bed early and get a good night's sleep.
- Get up early enough to make a leisurely trip to the place for the test – This way unforeseen events, traffic snarls, unfamiliar buildings, etc. will not upset you.
- Dress comfortably – A written test is not a fashion show. You will be known by number and not by name, so wear something comfortable.

- Leave excess paraphernalia at home – Shopping bags and odd bundles will get in your way. You need bring only the items mentioned in the official notice you received; usually everything you need is provided. Do not bring reference books to the exam. They will only confuse those last minutes and be taken away from you when in the test room.
- Arrive somewhat ahead of time – If because of transportation schedules you must get there very early, bring a newspaper or magazine to take your mind off yourself while waiting.
- Locate the examination room – When you have found the proper room, you will be directed to the seat or part of the room where you will sit. Sometimes you are given a sheet of instructions to read while you are waiting. Do not fill out any forms until you are told to do so; just read them and be prepared.
- Relax and prepare to listen to the instructions
- If you have any physical problem that may keep you from doing your best, be sure to tell the test administrator. If you are sick or in poor health, you really cannot do your best on the exam. You can come back and take the test some other time.

## VII. AT THE TEST

The day of the test is here and you have the test booklet in your hand. The temptation to get going is very strong. Caution! There is more to success than knowing the right answers. You must know how to identify your papers and understand variations in the type of short-answer question used in this particular examination. Follow these suggestions for maximum results from your efforts:

### 1) Cooperate with the monitor

The test administrator has a duty to create a situation in which you can be as much at ease as possible. He will give instructions, tell you when to begin, check to see that you are marking your answer sheet correctly, and so on. He is not there to guard you, although he will see that your competitors do not take unfair advantage. He wants to help you do your best.

### 2) Listen to all instructions

Don't jump the gun! Wait until you understand all directions. In most civil service tests you get more time than you need to answer the questions. So don't be in a hurry. Read each word of instructions until you clearly understand the meaning. Study the examples, listen to all announcements and follow directions. Ask questions if you do not understand what to do.

### 3) Identify your papers

Civil service exams are usually identified by number only. You will be assigned a number; you must not put your name on your test papers. Be sure to copy your number correctly. Since more than one exam may be given, copy your exact examination title.

### 4) Plan your time

Unless you are told that a test is a "speed" or "rate of work" test, speed itself is usually not important. Time enough to answer all the questions will be provided, but this does not mean that you have all day. An overall time limit has been set. Divide the total time (in minutes) by the number of questions to determine the approximate time you have for each question.

### 5) Do not linger over difficult questions

If you come across a difficult question, mark it with a paper clip (useful to have along) and come back to it when you have been through the booklet. One caution if you do this – be sure to skip a number on your answer sheet as well. Check often to be sure that you have not lost your place and that you are marking in the row numbered the same as the question you are answering.

### 6) Read the questions

Be sure you know what the question asks! Many capable people are unsuccessful because they failed to *read* the questions correctly.

### 7) Answer all questions

Unless you have been instructed that a penalty will be deducted for incorrect answers, it is better to guess than to omit a question.

### 8) Speed tests

It is often better NOT to guess on speed tests. It has been found that on timed tests people are tempted to spend the last few seconds before time is called in marking answers at random – without even reading them – in the hope of picking up a few extra points. To discourage this practice, the instructions may warn you that your score will be "corrected" for guessing. That is, a penalty will be applied. The incorrect answers will be deducted from the correct ones, or some other penalty formula will be used.

### 9) Review your answers

If you finish before time is called, go back to the questions you guessed or omitted to give them further thought. Review other answers if you have time.

### 10) Return your test materials

If you are ready to leave before others have finished or time is called, take ALL your materials to the monitor and leave quietly. Never take any test material with you. The monitor can discover whose papers are not complete, and taking a test booklet may be grounds for disqualification.

## VIII. EXAMINATION TECHNIQUES

1) Read the general instructions carefully. These are usually printed on the first page of the exam booklet. As a rule, these instructions refer to the timing of the examination; the fact that you should not start work until the signal and must stop work at a signal, etc. If there are any *special* instructions, such as a choice of questions to be answered, make sure that you note this instruction carefully.

2) When you are ready to start work on the examination, that is as soon as the signal has been given, read the instructions to each question booklet, underline any key words or phrases, such as *least, best, outline, describe* and the like. In this way you will tend to answer as requested rather than discover on reviewing your paper that you *listed without describing*, that you selected the *worst* choice rather than the *best* choice, etc.

3) If the examination is of the objective or multiple-choice type – that is, each question will also give a series of possible answers: A, B, C or D, and you are called upon to select the best answer and write the letter next to that answer on your answer paper – it is advisable to start answering each question in turn. There may be anywhere from 50 to 100 such questions in the three or four hours allotted and you can see how much time would be taken if you read through all the questions before beginning to answer any. Furthermore, if you come across a question or group of questions which you know would be difficult to answer, it would undoubtedly affect your handling of all the other questions.

4) If the examination is of the essay type and contains but a few questions, it is a moot point as to whether you should read all the questions before starting to answer any one. Of course, if you are given a choice – say five out of seven and the like – then it is essential to read all the questions so you can eliminate the two that are most difficult. If, however, you are asked to answer all the questions, there may be danger in trying to answer the easiest one first because you may find that you will spend too much time on it. The best technique is to answer the first question, then proceed to the second, etc.

5) Time your answers. Before the exam begins, write down the time it started, then add the time allowed for the examination and write down the time it must be completed, then divide the time available somewhat as follows:
   - If 3-1/2 hours are allowed, that would be 210 minutes. If you have 80 objective-type questions, that would be an average of 2-1/2 minutes per question. Allow yourself no more than 2 minutes per question, or a total of 160 minutes, which will permit about 50 minutes to review.
   - If for the time allotment of 210 minutes there are 7 essay questions to answer, that would average about 30 minutes a question. Give yourself only 25 minutes per question so that you have about 35 minutes to review.

6) The most important instruction is to *read each question* and make sure you know what is wanted. The second most important instruction is to *time yourself properly* so that you answer every question. The third most important instruction is to *answer every question*. Guess if you have to but include something for each question. Remember that you will receive no credit for a blank and will probably receive some credit if you write something in answer to an essay question. If you guess a letter – say "B" for a multiple-choice question – you may have guessed right. If you leave a blank as an answer to a multiple-choice question, the examiners may respect your feelings but it will not add a point to your score. Some exams may penalize you for wrong answers, so in such cases *only*, you may not want to guess unless you have some basis for your answer.

7) Suggestions
   a. Objective-type questions
      1. Examine the question booklet for proper sequence of pages and questions
      2. Read all instructions carefully
      3. Skip any question which seems too difficult; return to it after all other questions have been answered
      4. Apportion your time properly; do not spend too much time on any single question or group of questions

5. Note and underline key words – *all, most, fewest, least, best, worst, same, opposite,* etc.
6. Pay particular attention to negatives
7. Note unusual option, e.g., unduly long, short, complex, different or similar in content to the body of the question
8. Observe the use of "hedging" words – *probably, may, most likely,* etc.
9. Make sure that your answer is put next to the same number as the question
10. Do not second-guess unless you have good reason to believe the second answer is definitely more correct
11. Cross out original answer if you decide another answer is more accurate; do not erase until you are ready to hand your paper in
12. Answer all questions; guess unless instructed otherwise
13. Leave time for review

  b. Essay questions
   1. Read each question carefully
   2. Determine exactly what is wanted. Underline key words or phrases.
   3. Decide on outline or paragraph answer
   4. Include many different points and elements unless asked to develop any one or two points or elements
   5. Show impartiality by giving pros and cons unless directed to select one side only
   6. Make and write down any assumptions you find necessary to answer the questions
   7. Watch your English, grammar, punctuation and choice of words
   8. Time your answers; don't crowd material

8) Answering the essay question

Most essay questions can be answered by framing the specific response around several key words or ideas. Here are a few such key words or ideas:

M's: manpower, materials, methods, money, management
P's: purpose, program, policy, plan, procedure, practice, problems, pitfalls, personnel, public relations

  a. Six basic steps in handling problems:
   1. Preliminary plan and background development
   2. Collect information, data and facts
   3. Analyze and interpret information, data and facts
   4. Analyze and develop solutions as well as make recommendations
   5. Prepare report and sell recommendations
   6. Install recommendations and follow up effectiveness

  b. Pitfalls to avoid
   1. *Taking things for granted* – A statement of the situation does not necessarily imply that each of the elements is necessarily true; for example, a complaint may be invalid and biased so that all that can be taken for granted is that a complaint has been registered

2. *Considering only one side of a situation* – Wherever possible, indicate several alternatives and then point out the reasons you selected the best one
3. *Failing to indicate follow up* – Whenever your answer indicates action on your part, make certain that you will take proper follow-up action to see how successful your recommendations, procedures or actions turn out to be
4. *Taking too long in answering any single question* – Remember to time your answers properly

## IX. AFTER THE TEST

Scoring procedures differ in detail among civil service jurisdictions although the general principles are the same. Whether the papers are hand-scored or graded by machine we have described, they are nearly always graded by number. That is, the person who marks the paper knows only the number – never the name – of the applicant. Not until all the papers have been graded will they be matched with names. If other tests, such as training and experience or oral interview ratings have been given, scores will be combined. Different parts of the examination usually have different weights. For example, the written test might count 60 percent of the final grade, and a rating of training and experience 40 percent. In many jurisdictions, veterans will have a certain number of points added to their grades.

After the final grade has been determined, the names are placed in grade order and an eligible list is established. There are various methods for resolving ties between those who get the same final grade – probably the most common is to place first the name of the person whose application was received first. Job offers are made from the eligible list in the order the names appear on it. You will be notified of your grade and your rank as soon as all these computations have been made. This will be done as rapidly as possible.

People who are found to meet the requirements in the announcement are called "eligibles." Their names are put on a list of eligible candidates. An eligible's chances of getting a job depend on how high he stands on this list and how fast agencies are filling jobs from the list.

When a job is to be filled from a list of eligibles, the agency asks for the names of people on the list of eligibles for that job. When the civil service commission receives this request, it sends to the agency the names of the three people highest on this list. Or, if the job to be filled has specialized requirements, the office sends the agency the names of the top three persons who meet these requirements from the general list.

The appointing officer makes a choice from among the three people whose names were sent to him. If the selected person accepts the appointment, the names of the others are put back on the list to be considered for future openings.

That is the rule in hiring from all kinds of eligible lists, whether they are for typist, carpenter, chemist, or something else. For every vacancy, the appointing officer has his choice of any one of the top three eligibles on the list. This explains why the person whose name is on top of the list sometimes does not get an appointment when some of the persons lower on the list do. If the appointing officer chooses the second or third eligible, the No. 1 eligible does not get a job at once, but stays on the list until he is appointed or the list is terminated.

## X. HOW TO PASS THE INTERVIEW TEST

The examination for which you applied requires an oral interview test. You have already taken the written test and you are now being called for the interview test – the final part of the formal examination.

You may think that it is not possible to prepare for an interview test and that there are no procedures to follow during an interview. Our purpose is to point out some things you can do in advance that will help you and some good rules to follow and pitfalls to avoid while you are being interviewed.

*What is an interview supposed to test?*

The written examination is designed to test the technical knowledge and competence of the candidate; the oral is designed to evaluate intangible qualities, not readily measured otherwise, and to establish a list showing the relative fitness of each candidate – as measured against his competitors – for the position sought. Scoring is not on the basis of "right" and "wrong," but on a sliding scale of values ranging from "not passable" to "outstanding." As a matter of fact, it is possible to achieve a relatively low score without a single "incorrect" answer because of evident weakness in the qualities being measured.

Occasionally, an examination may consist entirely of an oral test – either an individual or a group oral. In such cases, information is sought concerning the technical knowledges and abilities of the candidate, since there has been no written examination for this purpose. More commonly, however, an oral test is used to supplement a written examination.

*Who conducts interviews?*

The composition of oral boards varies among different jurisdictions. In nearly all, a representative of the personnel department serves as chairman. One of the members of the board may be a representative of the department in which the candidate would work. In some cases, "outside experts" are used, and, frequently, a businessman or some other representative of the general public is asked to serve. Labor and management or other special groups may be represented. The aim is to secure the services of experts in the appropriate field.

However the board is composed, it is a good idea (and not at all improper or unethical) to ascertain in advance of the interview who the members are and what groups they represent. When you are introduced to them, you will have some idea of their backgrounds and interests, and at least you will not stutter and stammer over their names.

*What should be done before the interview?*

While knowledge about the board members is useful and takes some of the surprise element out of the interview, there is other preparation which is more substantive. It *is* possible to prepare for an oral interview – in several ways:

**1) Keep a copy of your application and review it carefully before the interview**

This may be the only document before the oral board, and the starting point of the interview. Know what education and experience you have listed there, and the sequence and dates of all of it. Sometimes the board will ask you to review the highlights of your experience for them; you should not have to hem and haw doing it.

**2) Study the class specification and the examination announcement**

Usually, the oral board has one or both of these to guide them. The qualities, characteristics or knowledges required by the position sought are stated in these documents. They offer valuable clues as to the nature of the oral interview. For example, if the job involves supervisory responsibilities, the announcement will usually indicate that knowledge of modern supervisory methods and the qualifications of the candidate as a supervisor will be tested. If so, you can expect such questions, frequently in the form of a hypothetical situation which you are expected to solve. NEVER go into an oral without knowledge of the duties and responsibilities of the job you seek.

### 3) Think through each qualification required

Try to visualize the kind of questions you would ask if you were a board member. How well could you answer them? Try especially to appraise your own knowledge and background in each area, *measured against the job sought*, and identify any areas in which you are weak. Be critical and realistic – do not flatter yourself.

### 4) Do some general reading in areas in which you feel you may be weak

For example, if the job involves supervision and your past experience has NOT, some general reading in supervisory methods and practices, particularly in the field of human relations, might be useful. Do NOT study agency procedures or detailed manuals. The oral board will be testing your understanding and capacity, not your memory.

### 5) Get a good night's sleep and watch your general health and mental attitude

You will want a clear head at the interview. Take care of a cold or any other minor ailment, and of course, no hangovers.

*What should be done on the day of the interview?*

Now comes the day of the interview itself. Give yourself plenty of time to get there. Plan to arrive somewhat ahead of the scheduled time, particularly if your appointment is in the fore part of the day. If a previous candidate fails to appear, the board might be ready for you a bit early. By early afternoon an oral board is almost invariably behind schedule if there are many candidates, and you may have to wait. Take along a book or magazine to read, or your application to review, but leave any extraneous material in the waiting room when you go in for your interview. In any event, relax and compose yourself.

The matter of dress is important. The board is forming impressions about you – from your experience, your manners, your attitude, and your appearance. Give your personal appearance careful attention. Dress your best, but not your flashiest. Choose conservative, appropriate clothing, and be sure it is immaculate. This is a business interview, and your appearance should indicate that you regard it as such. Besides, being well groomed and properly dressed will help boost your confidence.

Sooner or later, someone will call your name and escort you into the interview room. *This is it.* From here on you are on your own. It is too late for any more preparation. But remember, you asked for this opportunity to prove your fitness, and you are here because your request was granted.

*What happens when you go in?*

The usual sequence of events will be as follows: The clerk (who is often the board stenographer) will introduce you to the chairman of the oral board, who will introduce you to the other members of the board. Acknowledge the introductions before you sit down. Do not be surprised if you find a microphone facing you or a stenotypist sitting by. Oral interviews are usually recorded in the event of an appeal or other review.

Usually the chairman of the board will open the interview by reviewing the highlights of your education and work experience from your application – primarily for the benefit of the other members of the board, as well as to get the material into the record. Do not interrupt or comment unless there is an error or significant misinterpretation; if that is the case, do not hesitate. But do not quibble about insignificant matters. Also, he will usually ask you some question about your education, experience or your present job – partly to get you to start talking and to establish the interviewing "rapport." He may start the actual questioning, or turn it over to one of the other members. Frequently, each member undertakes the questioning on a particular area, one in which he is perhaps most competent, so you can expect each member to participate in the examination. Because time is limited, you may also expect some rather abrupt switches in the direction the questioning takes, so do not be upset by it. Normally, a board member will not pursue a single line of questioning unless he discovers a particular strength or weakness.

After each member has participated, the chairman will usually ask whether any member has any further questions, then will ask you if you have anything you wish to add. Unless you are expecting this question, it may floor you. Worse, it may start you off on an extended, extemporaneous speech. The board is not usually seeking more information. The question is principally to offer you a last opportunity to present further qualifications or to indicate that you have nothing to add. So, if you feel that a significant qualification or characteristic has been overlooked, it is proper to point it out in a sentence or so. Do not compliment the board on the thoroughness of their examination -- they have been sketchy, and you know it. If you wish, merely say, "No thank you, I have nothing further to add." This is a point where you can "talk yourself out" of a good impression or fail to present an important bit of information. Remember, *you close the interview yourself.*

The chairman will then say, "That is all, Mr. _____, thank you." Do not be startled; the interview is over, and quicker than you think. Thank him, gather your belongings and take your leave. Save your sigh of relief for the other side of the door.

*How to put your best foot forward*

Throughout this entire process, you may feel that the board individually and collectively is trying to pierce your defenses, seek out your hidden weaknesses and embarrass and confuse you. Actually, this is not true. They are obliged to make an appraisal of your qualifications for the job you are seeking, and they want to see you in your best light. Remember, they must interview all candidates and a non-cooperative candidate may become a failure in spite of their best efforts to bring out his qualifications. Here are 15 suggestions that will help you:

**1) Be natural – Keep your attitude confident, not cocky**

If you are not confident that you can do the job, do not expect the board to be. Do not apologize for your weaknesses, try to bring out your strong points. The board is interested in a positive, not negative, presentation. Cockiness will antagonize any board member and make him wonder if you are covering up a weakness by a false show of strength.

**2) Get comfortable, but don't lounge or sprawl**

Sit erectly but not stiffly. A careless posture may lead the board to conclude that you are careless in other things, or at least that you are not impressed by the importance of the occasion. Either conclusion is natural, even if incorrect. Do not fuss with your clothing, a pencil or an ashtray. Your hands may occasionally be useful to emphasize a point; do not let them become a point of distraction.

**3) Do not wisecrack or make small talk**

This is a serious situation, and your attitude should show that you consider it as such. Further, the time of the board is limited – they do not want to waste it, and neither should you.

**4) Do not exaggerate your experience or abilities**

In the first place, from information in the application or other interviews and sources, the board may know more about you than you think. Secondly, you probably will not get away with it. An experienced board is rather adept at spotting such a situation, so do not take the chance.

**5) If you know a board member, do not make a point of it, yet do not hide it**

Certainly you are not fooling him, and probably not the other members of the board. Do not try to take advantage of your acquaintanceship – it will probably do you little good.

**6) Do not dominate the interview**

Let the board do that. They will give you the clues – do not assume that you have to do all the talking. Realize that the board has a number of questions to ask you, and do not try to take up all the interview time by showing off your extensive knowledge of the answer to the first one.

**7) Be attentive**

You only have 20 minutes or so, and you should keep your attention at its sharpest throughout. When a member is addressing a problem or question to you, give him your undivided attention. Address your reply principally to him, but do not exclude the other board members.

**8) Do not interrupt**

A board member may be stating a problem for you to analyze. He will ask you a question when the time comes. Let him state the problem, and wait for the question.

**9) Make sure you understand the question**

Do not try to answer until you are sure what the question is. If it is not clear, restate it in your own words or ask the board member to clarify it for you. However, do not haggle about minor elements.

**10) Reply promptly but not hastily**

A common entry on oral board rating sheets is "candidate responded readily," or "candidate hesitated in replies." Respond as promptly and quickly as you can, but do not jump to a hasty, ill-considered answer.

**11) Do not be peremptory in your answers**

A brief answer is proper – but do not fire your answer back. That is a losing game from your point of view. The board member can probably ask questions much faster than you can answer them.

**12) Do not try to create the answer you think the board member wants**

He is interested in what kind of mind you have and how it works – not in playing games. Furthermore, he can usually spot this practice and will actually grade you down on it.

**13) Do not switch sides in your reply merely to agree with a board member**

Frequently, a member will take a contrary position merely to draw you out and to see if you are willing and able to defend your point of view. Do not start a debate, yet do not surrender a good position. If a position is worth taking, it is worth defending.

### 14) Do not be afraid to admit an error in judgment if you are shown to be wrong

The board knows that you are forced to reply without any opportunity for careful consideration. Your answer may be demonstrably wrong. If so, admit it and get on with the interview.

### 15) Do not dwell at length on your present job

The opening question may relate to your present assignment. Answer the question but do not go into an extended discussion. You are being examined for a *new* job, not your present one. As a matter of fact, try to phrase ALL your answers in terms of the job for which you are being examined.

*Basis of Rating*

Probably you will forget most of these "do's" and "don'ts" when you walk into the oral interview room. Even remembering them all will not ensure you a passing grade. Perhaps you did not have the qualifications in the first place. But remembering them will help you to put your best foot forward, without treading on the toes of the board members.

Rumor and popular opinion to the contrary notwithstanding, an oral board wants you to make the best appearance possible. They know you are under pressure – but they also want to see how you respond to it as a guide to what your reaction would be under the pressures of the job you seek. They will be influenced by the degree of poise you display, the personal traits you show and the manner in which you respond.

## ABOUT THIS BOOK

This book contains tests divided into Examination Sections. Go through each test, answering every question in the margin. We have also attached a sample answer sheet at the back of the book that can be removed and used. At the end of each test look at the answer key and check your answers. On the ones you got wrong, look at the right answer choice and learn. Do not fill in the answers first. Do not memorize the questions and answers, but understand the answer and principles involved. On your test, the questions will likely be different from the samples. Questions are changed and new ones added. If you understand these past questions you should have success with any changes that arise. Tests may consist of several types of questions. We have additional books on each subject should more study be advisable or necessary for you. Finally, the more you study, the better prepared you will be. This book is intended to be the last thing you study before you walk into the examination room. Prior study of relevant texts is also recommended. NLC publishes some of these in our Fundamental Series. Knowledge and good sense are important factors in passing your exam. Good luck also helps. So now study this Passbook, absorb the material contained within and take that knowledge into the examination. Then do your best to pass that exam.

# EXAMINATION SECTION

# EXAMINATION SECTION
# TEST 1

DIRECTIONS: Each question or incomplete statement is followed by several suggested answers or completions. Select the one that BEST answers the question or completes the statement. *PRINT THE LETTER OF THE CORRECT ANSWER IN THE SPACE AT THE RIGHT.*

1. Which of the following factors contributes MOST to infant mortality?   1_____

    A. Motor vehicle accidents
    B. Congenital cardiac malformation
    C. Prematurity
    D. Acute renal failure
    E. Pneumonia

2. All of the following statements are true regarding tuberculosis in the United States EXCEPT:   2_____

    A. Mortality and morbidity rates increase with age
    B. Mortality rates are higher for males than females
    C. The incidence is much higher among the poor than the rich
    D. In low incidence areas, such as the United States, most tuberculosis is exogenous
    E. In 2015, the reported incidence of clinical disease in the United States was 3.0/100,000 population

3. Tubercle bacilli CANNOT be destroyed by   3_____

    A. heat              B. cold
    C. ultraviolet light  D. phenol
    E. tricresol solution

4. The MOST frequent reservoirs for tuberculosis disease are   4_____

    A. badgers    B. mosquitoes    C. humans
    D. cats       E. deer

5. The LEADING cause of death for people younger than age 65 in the United States is   5_____

    A. heart disease
    B. cerebrovascular disease
    C. chronic obstructive pulmonary disease
    D. diabetes mellitus
    E. chronic liver disease

6. Cooling towers and air conditioning units serve as breeding grounds for   6_____

    A. staphylococcus aureus
    B. klebsiella pneumoniae
    C. streptococcus pneumoniae
    D. L. pneumophilia
    E. histoplasma capsulatum

7. Diseases transmitted by mosquitoes, mites, and ticks can be prevented by all of the following precautions EXCEPT

    A. protective clothing
    B. mask and gloves
    C. insect repellents
    D. door and window screens
    E. more than one but not all of the above

8. The PRINCIPAL area of study in injury control is

    A. epidemiology
    B. prevention
    C. treatment
    D. rehabilitation
    E. all of the above

9. Benzene is MOST likely to be associated with _____ cancer.

    A. blood
    B. kidney
    C. liver
    D. brain
    E. bone

10. A _____ test is used when the patient's wishes can be inferred from his or her known religious, ethical, and/or lifestyle beliefs.

    A. subjective
    B. relative
    C. limited objective
    D. pure objective
    E. none of the above

11. It is NOT true that standard deviation

    A. is the positive square root of variance
    B. is the most useful measure of dispersion
    C. standardizes extreme values
    D. decreases when the sample size increases
    E. of a small size in a sample causes the sample mean to be close to each individual value

12. The difference between the highest and lowest values in a series is called the

    A. range
    B. variance
    C. standard deviation
    D. coefficient of variation
    E. none of the above

13. The ratio of the standard deviation of a series to the arithmetic mean of the series is known as the

    A. coefficient of variation
    B. range
    C. variance
    D. frequency
    E. prevalence

14. In a disease which is usually of acute onset, lasts a couple of weeks, and has a case fatality rate of 75 to 85%, the

    A. prevalence is always higher than that of annual incidence
    B. incidence is always higher than the prevalence
    C. prevalence and annual incidence are always equal
    D. mortality rate will be consistently high in all countries where the disease occurs
    E. none of the above

15. A random sample of 20,000 men is screened for a history of excessive sugar consumption and the presence of diabetes.
    This is called a _____ study.

    A. prospective
    B. historical
    C. cross-sectional population
    D. retrospective-prospective
    E. case control retrospective

16. Five hundred young adults who are known cocaine users are assembled together with a control group. Recognizable psychotics are excluded, and the remainder are followed for 3 years to see whether any psychoses develop in them.
    This is a _____ study.

    A. retrospective
    B. case control retrospective
    C. cross-sectional population
    D. cohort
    E. none of the above

17. The FIRST and most important thing for the epidemiologist to do during the investigation of a patient with a communicable disease is to investigate

    A. the first source of infection
    B. the mode of transmission
    C. how many people have been infected
    D. the accuracy of the diagnosis
    E. preventive control of the disease

18. The single MOST important measure for the prevention of typhoid fever in a community is

    A. a ceftriaxon prophylaxis for all persons who are exposed to the disease
    B. washing hands
    C. immunization of the high risk population
    D. hospitalization and treatment of all known carriers
    E. water purification

19. Diseases more likely to occur in women than in men include all of the following EXCEPT

    A. Raynaud's disease
    B. sarcoidosis
    C. gout
    D. systemic lupus erythematosus
    E. secondary hypothyroidism

20. Over the past 50 years, which of the following chronic conditions has experienced the greatest decline in mortality rate?

    A. Heart disease
    B. Stroke
    C. Cancer
    D. Pneumonia
    E. Influenza

21. The population having the HIGHEST frequency of thalassemia is the

   A. Jews
   B. Italians
   C. Chinese
   D. Japanese
   E. Americans

22. Over the past ten years, the majority of individuals who were initially diagnosed with diabetes mellitus were in what age group?

   A. 18-29
   B. 30-39
   C. 50-59
   D. 70-79
   E. 80-89

23. Of the following, the disease LARGELY confined to people born in temperate climate zones and manifested in early adult life is

   A. diabetes
   B. multiple sclerosis
   C. thalassemia
   D. hypertension
   E. prostate cancer

24. Hepatitis A has the highest incidence rate in individuals in which age group?

   A. 0-9
   B. 10-19
   C. 20-29
   D. 30-39
   E. 50-59

25. Recurrent episodes of low grade fever and arthralgia FREQUENTLY affect workers in

   A. slaughter houses
   B. cotton mills
   C. coal mines
   D. hospital laboratories
   E. none of the above

## KEY (CORRECT ANSWERS)

| | | | |
|---|---|---|---|
| 1. C | | 11. C |
| 2. D | | 12. A |
| 3. B | | 13. A |
| 4. C | | 14. B |
| 5. A | | 15. C |
| 6. D | | 16. D |
| 7. B | | 17. D |
| 8. E | | 18. E |
| 9. A | | 19. C |
| 10. C | | 20. B |

21. B
22. C
23. B
24. C
25. A

# TEST 2

DIRECTIONS: Each question or incomplete statement is followed by several suggested answers or completions. Select the one that BEST answers the question or completes the statement. *PRINT THE LETTER OF THE CORRECT ANSWER IN THE SPACE AT THE RIGHT.*

1. Risk factors for malignancies of the liver and intra-hepatic biliary tract may include all of the following EXCEPT       1_____

    A. alpha-1 antitrypsin deficiency
    B. aflatoxin
    C. gentamicin
    D. alcohol
    E. steroids

2. The parasite associated with an increased risk for developing carcinoma of the biliary tree is       2_____

    A. ascaris lumbricoides        B. balantidium coli
    C. cryptoporidium              D. colonorchis sinensis
    E. enterobias vermicular is

3. Of the following, the immunization that should NOT be given to an individual who has received immune globulin within the previous 3 months is       3_____

    A. IPV       B. DTP       C. MMR
    D. HBIG      E. none of the above

4. Which of the following is the LEADING cause of maternal death among pregnancies with abortive outcomes?       4_____

    A. Rubella              B. Ectopic pregnancy
    C. Teratoma             D. Defective germ cell
    E. Herpes simplex II

5. All of the following are leading causes of maternal mortality in the United States EXCEPT       5_____

    A. anesthesia complication
    B. embolism
    C. hypertensive disease of pregnancy
    D. hemorrhage
    E. maternal age between 20 and 30

6. _____ is NOT a reportable disease.       6_____

    A. Pulmonary tuberculosis       B. Mumps
    C. Measles                      D. Choriomeningitis
    E. Meningococcal sepsis

7. The scientific field dealing with the collection, classification, description, analysis, interpretation, and presentation of data is called       7_____

    A. distributions         B. statistics
    C. standard deviation    D. median
    E. cohort study

8. What type of treatment regimen should be administered to an infant born to a mother with active gonorrhea?

   A. Single IM dose of ceftriaxone
   B. Single oral dose of azithromycin
   C. Dual therapy of ceftriaxone and azithromycin
   D. Dual therapy of ceftriaxone and spectinomycin
   E. None of the above

9. A precaution necessary for children in day care who have pneumococcal disease is _____ isolation.

   A. strict        B. contact         C. enteric
   D. respiratory   E. none of the above

10. Children who have ever had a life-threatening allergic reaction to _____ should not get the polio vaccine.

    A. gluten       B. peanuts        C. eggs
    D. antibiotics  E. pollen

11. Stillbirths or perinatal death is a result of _____ % of pregnancies in women with untreated early syphilis.

    A. 5    B. 10    C. 25    D. 40    E. 80

12. Strongyloidiasis is endemic in the tropics and subtropics, including the southern and southwestern United States. The single MOST important control measure is

    A. purification of water
    B. food cooked at a higher temperature
    C. sanitary disposal measure for human waste
    D. mass vaccination of exposed population
    E. detection and treatment of all infected persons

13. In a large population, the mode of transmission MOST difficult to prevent is _____ spread.

    A. vector       B. person to person
    C. airborne     D. droplet
    E. none of the above

14. Of the following, the factor contributing the MOST to infant mortality is

    A. seizures              B. prematurity       C. hypothyroidism
    D. congenital heart disease   E. birth trauma

15. Point prevalence studies tend to have an over-representation of

    A. chronic cases      B. fatal cases       C. short-term cases
    D. healthy persons    E. all of the above

16. The PRIMARY function of the federal government in the Medicaid program is to

    A. set standards
    B. provide services in their own institutions *only*
    C. investigate *only* services rendered
    D. pay for services
    E. pay for nursing care *only*

Questions 17-21.

DIRECTIONS: In Questions 17 through 21, match the numbered description with the appropriate lettered term listed in Column I. Place the letter of the correct answer in the space at the right.

COLUMN I
A. Sensitivity
B. Specificity
C. Screening
D. Median
E. Mode

17. The MOST commonly occurring value in a series of values 17_____

18. The initial examination of an individual whose disease is not yet under medical care 18_____

19. May be calculated in an ongoing longevity study 19_____

20. The ability of a screening test to identify correctly those individuals who truly have the disease 20_____

21. The ability of a test to identify correctly those individuals who truly do not have the disease 21_____

Questions 22-25.

DIRECTIONS: In Questions 22 through 25, match the numbered definition with the appropriate lettered term listed in Column I. Place the letter of the correct answer in the space at the right.

COLUMN I
A. Efficiency
B. Validity
C. Reliability
D. Bias
E. Causality

22. The extent to which a test provides the same result on the same subject on two or more occasions 22_____

23. The extent to which the results of a test agree with the results of another test that is accepted as more accurate or closer to the truth 23_____

24. A systematic error that is unintentionally made 24_____

25. Denotes direct effect 25_____

# KEY (CORRECT ANSWERS)

1. C
2. D
3. C
4. B
5. E

6. D
7. B
8. C
9. E
10. D

11. D
12. C
13. C
14. B
15. C

16. D
17. E
18. C
19. D
20. A

21. B
22. C
23. B
24. D
25. E

# EXAMINATION SECTION
# TEST 1

DIRECTIONS: Each question or incomplete statement is followed by several suggested answers or completions. Select the one that BEST answers the question or completes the statement. *PRINT THE LETTER OF THE CORRECT ANSWER IN THE SPACE AT THE RIGHT.*

Questions 1-4.

DIRECTIONS: Questions 1 through 4 are to be answered on the basis of the following information.

In a day care center of 30 children (20 females and 10 males), 7 boys develop hepatitis A over a 3-week period. During the next 8 weeks, an additional 2 boys and 5 girls develop the infection.

1. The attack rate of hepatitis A in this day care center is _____%.
    A. 20    B. 30    C. 40    D. 46.6    E. 54.5

2. The secondary attack rate of hepatitis A in this day care center is MOST NEARLY _____%.
    A. 20    B. 15    C. 23    D. 27    E. 10

3. The attack rate of hepatitis A for boys in this school is MOST NEARLY _____%.
    A. 16    B. 40    C. 50    D. 60    E. 64

4. The attack rate of hepatitis A for girls is MOST NEARLY _____%.
    A. 21    B. 24    C. 25    D. 27    E. 30

5. The epidemic curve suggests a common source outbreak with
    A. continuing common source outbreak
    B. fecal-oral transmission
    C. secondary airborne transmission
    D. secondary person-to-person transmission
    E. none of the above

6. The _____ rate is determined by the number of deaths caused by a specific disease divided by the number of cases of the disease.
    A. mortality              B. case fatality
    C. attack                 D. cause specific death
    E. none of the above

7. Rate is the expression of the probability of occurrence of a particular event in a defined population during a specified period of time.
The rate calculated for various segments of the population is known as the _____ rate.
    A. specific               B. crude
    C. adjusted               D. variable
    E. none of the above

8. The sources of disease surveillance data include all of the following EXCEPT

   A. individual case reports
   B. emergency room visit records
   C. hospital discharge summaries
   D. death certificates
   E. none of the above

9. All of the following are true about tularemia EXCEPT that it is

   A. a zoonotic disease
   B. more common during the summer months in the western states
   C. more common in winter months in the eastern states
   D. primarily transmitted by the bite of a spider
   E. none of the above

10. Which of the following is NOT among the basic steps in an investigation of an epidemic?

    A. Verification of diagnosis
    B. Establishing the existence of an epidemic
    C. Characterization of the distribution of cases
    D. Formulating a conclusion
    E. All of the above

11. The LAST step in conducting an epidemic investigation is to

    A. develop an hypothesis
    B. test the hypothesis
    C. formulate a conclusion
    D. institute control measures
    E. establish the diagnosis of an epidemic

12. The patients who are infected with an agent but never develop clinical symptoms of the disease are known as _____ carriers.

    A. incubatory          B. subclinical          C. chronic
    D. convalescent        E. clinical

13. All of the following are uses of epidemiology EXCEPT to

    A. identify factors that cause disease
    B. explain how and why diseases and epidemics occur
    C. establish a clinical diagnosis of disease
    D. determine a patient's prognosis
    E. evaluate the effectiveness of health programs

14. The biological traits that determine the occurrence of a disease include all of the following EXCEPT

    A. genetic characteristics          B. diet
    C. race                             D. ethnic origin
    E. sex

15. The general factors of resistance in a human host include all of the following EXCEPT

   A. the immune system
   B. intact skin
   C. diarrhea
   D. normal bacterial flora
   E. gastric juices

16. All of the following are examples of direct contact transmission EXCEPT

   A. syphilis
   B. herpes
   C. hepatitis B
   D. sporotrichosis
   E. none of the above

17. The basic aims and specific goals of medical studies and clinical research do NOT include

   A. assessing health status or clinical characteristics
   B. eliminating all carriers of diseases
   C. determining and assessing treatment outcomes
   D. identifying and assessing risk factors
   E. all of the above

18. Incidence and prevalence studies usually concern all of the following EXCEPT

   A. the occurrence of disease
   B. a comparison of outcomes between different treatments
   C. adverse side effects of drugs
   D. the death rate for a certain disease
   E. none of the above

19. A case series report can address almost any clinical issue but it is MOST commonly used to describe

   A. clinical characteristics of a disease
   B. screening test results
   C. treatment outcomes
   D. an unexpected result or event
   E. none of the above

20. A comparison of chemotherapy to chemotherapy plus radiation for laryngeal carcinoma would be an appropriate topic for a(n)

   A. cohort study
   B. case control study
   C. clinical trial
   D. case series report
   E. incidence and prevalence study

21. The sum of all values in a series divided by the actual number of values in the series is known as the

   A. mode
   B. median
   C. geometric mean
   D. arithmetic mean
   E. none of the above

22. The MOST commonly occurring value in a series of values is the   22.____

    A. mode
    B. median
    C. geometric mean
    D. arithmetic mean
    E. none of the above

23. The ratio of the standard deviation of a series to the arithmetic mean of the series is known as the   23.____

    A. range
    B. variance
    C. coefficient of variation
    D. standard deviation
    E. epidemic curve

24. The sum of squared deviations from the mean divided by the number of values in the series minus 1 is called the   24.____

    A. range
    B. variance
    C. standard deviation
    D. coefficient of variation
    E. frequency polygon

25. The _____ is a tool for comparing categories of mutually exclusive discrete data.   25.____

    A. pie chart
    B. Venn diagram
    C. bar diagram
    D. histogram
    E. frequency polygon

# KEY (CORRECT ANSWERS)

| | | | |
|---|---|---|---|
| 1. D | | 11. D | |
| 2. C | | 12. B | |
| 3. E | | 13. D | |
| 4. C | | 14. B | |
| 5. D | | 15. A | |
| 6. B | | 16. E | |
| 7. A | | 17. B | |
| 8. E | | 18. B | |
| 9. D | | 19. A | |
| 10. E | | 20. C | |

21. D
22. A
23. C
24. B
25. C

# TEST 2

DIRECTIONS: Each question or incomplete statement is followed by several suggested answers or completions. Select the one that BEST answers the question or completes the statement. *PRINT THE LETTER OF THE CORRECT ANSWER IN THE SPACE AT THE RIGHT.*

1. A _____ is a special form of the bar diagram used to represent categories of continuous and ordered data.

    A. pie chart
    B. histogram
    C. Venn diagram
    D. cumulative frequency graph
    E. frequency polygon

2. A medical student performs venipuncture on 1,000 randomly selected patients and is successful on the first attempt 700 times.
What is the probability that her next venipuncture will be successful on the first attempt?

    A. 7%    B. 14%    C. 50%    D. 70%    E. 80%

3. All of the following are true regarding the standard error of the mean of a sample EXCEPT that it

    A. is an estimate of the standard deviation of the population
    B. is based on a normal distribution
    C. increases as the sample size increases
    D. is used to determine confidence limits
    E. none of the above

4. All of the following are characteristics of a confidence interval EXCEPT that it

    A. is based on a critical ratio when the sample is large
    B. gives an indication of the likely magnitude of the true value
    C. gives an indication of the certainty of the point estimate
    D. becomes narrower as the sample size increases
    E. none of the above

5. Nonparametric tests can be used to compare two populations with which of the following conditions?

    A. Each population is unimodal
    B. Both populations have equal numbers
    C. Each population is independent
    D. Each population is distributed normally
    E. All of the above

6. All of the following vaccines are grown in embryonated chicken eggs EXCEPT

    A. yellow fever    B. measles    C. mumps
    D. rubella         E. influenza

7. Which of the following vaccines should NOT be given to individuals who live in households with an immuno-compromised host?

    A. Yellow fever
    B. Hepatitis B
    C. Oral polio
    D. Influenza
    E. Diphtheriae

8. A solution of antibodies derived from the serum of animals immunized with a specific antigen is a(n)

    A. immunoglobulin
    B. antitoxin
    C. toxoid
    D. vaccine
    E. none of the above

9. All of the following may be significant sequale of measles infection EXCEPT

    A. pneumonia
    B. encephalitis
    C. congenital birth defects
    D. mental retardation
    E. death

10. All of the following statements about vaccination during pregnancy are true EXCEPT:

    A. Live attenuated viral vaccines should not be given to pregnant women
    B. Pregnant women at substantial risk of exposure may receive a live viral vaccine
    C. There is evidence that inactivated vaccines also pose risks to the fetus
    D. There is no evidence that immunoglobulins pose any risk to the fetus
    E. None of the above

11. None of the following conditions are reasons for delaying or discontinuing routine immunizations EXCEPT

    A. soreness, redness or swelling at the injection site in reaction to previous immunization
    B. a temperature of more than 105F in reaction to previous DTP vaccine
    C. mild diarrheal illness in an otherwise well child
    D. current antimicrobial therapy
    E. breastfeeding

12. Children and infants with any of the following disorders should not receive pertussis vaccine EXCEPT those with

    A. uncontrolled epilepsy
    B. infantile spasms
    C. progressive encephalopathy
    D. developmental delay
    E. none of the above

13. Which of the following groups of patients should NOT receive pneumococcal polysaccharide vaccine?

    A. Elderly, age 65 or older
    B. Immunocompromised
    C. Children age 2 years or older with anatomic or functional asplenia

D. Children age 2 years or older with nephrotic syndrome or CSF leaks
E. Children under 2 years of age

14. All of the following are significant complications of sexually transmitted diseases in women EXCEPT

    A. pelvic inflammatory disease
    B. infertility
    C. teratogenicity
    D. cancer
    E. ectopic pregnancy

14.____

15. For primary prevention and maximal safety, a person should

    A. engage in a mutually monogamous relationship
    B. limit the number of sexual partners
    C. inspect and question new partners
    D. avoid sexual practices involving anal or fecal contact
    E. all of the above

15.____

16. All of the following are complications caused by untreated syphilis infection EXCEPT

    A. obesity           B. blindness
    C. psychosis         D. cardiovascular disease
    E. none of the above

16.____

17. All of the following statements are true regarding syphilis EXCEPT:

    A. The organism cannot enter through intact skin
    B. Everyone is susceptible
    C. There is no natural or acquired immunity
    D. No vaccine is available
    E. Reinfection is rare

17.____

18. Which of the following sexually transmitted diseases rank as the number one reported communicable disease in the United States?

    A. Syphilis          B. Gonorrhea         C. AIDS
    D. Chlamydia         E. Hepatitis B

18.____

19. Which of the following is believed to be the MOST common sexually transmitted bacterial pathogen in the United States?

    A. Treponema pallidum        B. Chlamydia trachomatis
    C. Nisseriae gonorrhea       D. E. coli
    E. Herpes zoster

19.____

20. All of the following are documented modes of transmission for human immunodeficiency virus EXCEPT _____ transmission.

    A. sexual            B. percutaneous exposure
    C. airborne          D. mother to child
    E. none of the above

20.____

21. In order to prevent HIV infection, which of the following groups should NOT donate blood?

    A. Any man who has had sexual contact with another man since 1977
    B. Present or past IV drug abusers
    C. Individuals from Central Africa and Haiti
    D. Sexual partners of any of the above groups
    E. All of the above

22. Chlamydia trachomatis, the causative agent of chlamydia infection, has all of the following characteristics EXCEPT it

    A. grows only intracellularly
    B. contains both DNA and RNA
    C. is a protozoa
    D. divides by binary fission
    E. has cell walls similar to gram-negative bacteriae

23. All of the following are true regarding the resultant effects of chlamydia trachomatis EXCEPT:

    A. Approximately 50% cases of non-gonococcal urethritis in men
    B. 99% of cases of pelvic inflammatory disease
    C. Mucopurulent cervicitis
    D. Inclusion conjunctivitis in infants born to infected mothers
    E. Acute epididymitis in men

24. All of the following statements are true regarding hepatitis A infection EXCEPT:

    A. Approximately 70% of Americans are infected by the age of 20
    B. Incidence appears to be declining
    C. Infection is related to age and socioeconomic status
    D. The incubation period is 15-50 days with an average of 28-30 days
    E. Young children are more likely to have subclinical infections

25. The transmission of hepatitis A virus is facilitated by all of the following EXCEPT

    A. poor personal hygiene
    B. poor sanitation
    C. drinking out of the same cup
    D. eating uncooked or raw food
    E. eating food contaminated by human hands after cooking

# KEY (CORRECT ANSWERS)

|   |   |   |   |
|---|---|---|---|
| 1. | B | 11. | B |
| 2. | D | 12. | D |
| 3. | C | 13. | E |
| 4. | E | 14. | C |
| 5. | E | 15. | E |
| 6. | D | 16. | A |
| 7. | C | 17. | E |
| 8. | B | 18. | B |
| 9. | C | 19. | B |
| 10. | C | 20. | C |

21. E
22. C
23. B
24. A
25. C

# EXAMINATION SECTION
# TEST 1

DIRECTIONS: Each question or incomplete statement is followed by several suggested answers or completions. Select the one that BEST answers the question or completes the statement. *PRINT THE LETTER OF THE CORRECT ANSWER IN THE SPACE AT THE RIGHT.*

1. A PPD reaction of greater than or equal to 5 mm induration is considered positive in all of the following individuals EXCEPT

    A. persons with HIV infection
    B. IV drug abusers who are HIV antibody negative
    C. close recent contacts of an infectious tuberculosis case
    D. persons with a chest radiograph consistent with old, healed tuberculosis
    E. persons with HIV infection or with risk factors for HIV infection who have an unknown IV antibody status

1.____

2. All of the following are true about tuberculosis EXCEPT:

    A. The causative agent is M. tuberculosis var. hominis
    B. It is more likely to occur in older individuals (more than 45 years of age)
    C. It is more common in non-whites than in whites
    D. It is more common in men than in women
    E. About 90% of cases in the United States represent new infections

2.____

3. The groups that should benefit from preventive therapy for tuberculosis include all of the following EXCEPT

    A. individuals whose skin test has converted from negative to positive in the previous 2 years
    B. individuals with positive mantoux test and with HIV infection
    C. tuberculin-negative IV drug abusers
    D. tuberculin-positive individuals under 35 years of age
    E. individuals with immunosuppressive therapy who are tuberculin positive

3.____

4. INH prophylaxis should not be used in any of the following EXCEPT in

    A. the presence of clinical disease
    B. a pregnant woman who has recently converted to tuberculin positive
    C. patients with unstable hepatic function
    D. individuals who were previously adequately treated
    E. individuals with a previous adverse reaction to INH

4.____

5. What is the MOST common cause of bacterial meningitis in children under age 5?

    A. Streptococcus pneumoniae
    B. H. influenza
    C. N. meningitidis
    D. E. coli
    E. Staphylococcus aureus

5.____

6. All of the following are true about H. influenza infection EXCEPT:

    A. Peak incidence is from age 3 months to 2 years
    B. The mortality rate is about 5%
    C. Secondary spread to day care contacts under 4 years of age is rare
    D. About two-thirds of the cases occur in children under 15 months of age
    E. None of the above

7. All of the following statements are true about hemophilus influenza type B infection EXCEPT:

    A. Rifampin is the drug of choice for chemoprophylaxis
    B. Rifampin may be given to pregnant women
    C. The disease is more common in native and black Americans
    D. Humans are the reservoir of infections
    E. None of the above

8. All of the following statements are true about meningococcal meningitis EXCEPT:

    A. It is the second most common cause of bacterial meningitis in the United States
    B. The peak incidence is around age 6-12 months
    C. Most cases occur in late winter and early spring
    D. The portal of entry is not the nasopharynx
    E. It is more likely to occur in newly aggregated young adults who are living in institutions and barracks

9. Antimicrobial chemoprophylaxis is the chief preventive measure in sporadic cases of meningococcal meningitis and should be offered to

    A. household contacts
    B. day care center contacts
    C. medical personnel who resuscitated, intubated or suctioned the patient before antibiotics were instituted
    D. all patients who were treated for meningococcal disease before discharge from the hospital
    E. all of the above

10. What is the MOST common cause of bacterial meningitis in children under 5 years of age?

    A. Streptococcus pneumoniae
    B. Nisseriae meningitidis
    C. Listeria monocytogenes
    D. Group B streptococcus
    E. Hemophilus influenza type B

11. All of the following are true about coronary heart disease EXCEPT:

    A. It is the leading cause of death in the United States
    B. About 4.6 million Americans have coronary heart disease
    C. It is most common in white men
    D. Women have a greater risk of myocardial infarction and sudden death
    E. Women have a greater risk of angina pectoris

12. According to the National Cholesterol Education Panel, which of the following is NOT a major risk factor for coronary artery disease?

    A. Women 55 years and older
    B. Hypertension
    C. Individuals with diabetes mellitus
    D. High density lipoprotein (HDL) less than 35 mg/dl
    E. Obesity

13. The number one cause of cancer death in the United States is _____ cancer.

    A. lung           B. breast         C. colorectal
    D. cervical       E. prostatic

14. The MOST common cancer in American men is _____ cancer.

    A. lung           B. breast         C. prostate
    D. colon          E. esophageal

15. All of the following are risk factors for women to develop breast cancer EXCEPT

    A. exposure to ionizing radiation
    B. becoming pregnant for the first time after age 30
    C. mother and sisters having breast cancer
    D. high socioeconomic status
    E. late menarchae

16. Cervical cancer is one of the leading causes of death among women. Of the following, which is NOT a risk factor for developing cervical cancer?

    A. Multiple sexual partners
    B. First coitus before age 20
    C. Low socioeconomic status
    D. Oral contraceptive use
    E. Partners of uncircumcised men

17. Population subgroups at INCREASED risk of developing anemia include

    A. women          B. elderly men
    C. children       D. blacks
    E. all of the above

18. Uncontrolled hypertensive disease increases the risk of developing all of the following disorders EXCEPT

    A. coronary heart disease     B. diabetes mellitus
    C. renal disease              D. cerebrovascular disease
    E. none of the above

19. All of the following statements are true regarding chronic obstructive pulmonary disease (COPD) EXCEPT:

    A. Men are at higher risk than women
    B. An estimated 16 million Americans have chronic bronchitis, asthma or emphysema
    C. The risk is related to the duration of smoking only

D. The risk is related to the number of cigarettes smoked daily and to the duration of smoking
E. Offspring of affected individuals are at higher risk

20. Which of the following statements is TRUE regarding diabetes in the United States?   20.____

    A. It accounts for 5% of all deaths.
    B. Its prevalence is estimated at 15%.
    C. 80% of all diabetics have the non-insulin dependent type.
    D. It is the leading cause of blindness.
    E. Men are at greater risk than women.

21. People with increased risk for suicide include all of the following EXCEPT   21.____

    A. drug users              B. married individuals
    C. teenagers               D. chronically depressed
    E. homosexuals

22. Conditions associated with an increased risk for suicide include all of the following EXCEPT   22.____

    A. unemployed
    B. seriously physically ill or handicapped
    C. chronically mentally ill
    D. substance abusers
    E. none of the above

23. The leading cause of death among black men aged 15-24 years is   23.____

    A. automobile accidents    B. homicide
    C. cancer                  D. drug abuse
    E. AIDS

24. All of the following are true regarding pernicious anemia EXCEPT:   24.____

    A. It primarily affects individuals over the age of 30
    B. The incidence increases with age
    C. It is more common in Asians and blacks
    D. It is caused by a vitamin $B_{12}$ deficiency
    E. None of the above

25. Which of the following groups of individuals have a high risk of injuries?   25.____

    A. Factory workers
    B. Alcoholics
    C. Individuals with osteoporosis
    D. Homeless
    E. All of the above

## KEY (CORRECT ANSWERS)

| | | | |
|---|---|---|---|
| 1. | B | 11. | D |
| 2. | E | 12. | D |
| 3. | C | 13. | A |
| 4. | B | 14. | C |
| 5. | B | 15. | E |
| 6. | C | 16. | C |
| 7. | B | 17. | E |
| 8. | D | 18. | B |
| 9. | E | 19. | C |
| 10. | E | 20. | D |

21. B
22. E
23. B
24. C
25. E

# TEST 2

DIRECTIONS: Each question or incomplete statement is followed by several suggested answers or completions. Select the one that BEST answers the question or completes the statement. *PRINT THE LETTER OF THE CORRECT ANSWER IN THE SPACE AT THE RIGHT.*

1. Which of the following factors does NOT increase a woman's risk of an ectopic pregnancy?   1._____

    A. Progestin exposure
    B. Pelvic inflammatory disease
    C. Smoking
    D. Use of alcohol
    E. Infertility

2. Breastfeeding usually enhances all of the following EXCEPT   2._____

    A. bonding between mother and infant
    B. infant nutrition
    C. immune defenses
    D. antibody response against HIV virus
    E. return of uterus to prepregnant size

3. Which of the following is NOT a leading cause of maternal mortality in the United States?   3._____

    A. Hypertensive disease of pregnancy
    B. Cardiovascular accidents
    C. Miscarriage
    D. Anesthesia complications
    E. All of the above

4. A well-woman prenatal visit should include all of the following EXCEPT a(n)   4._____

    A. weight check
    B. blood pressure check
    C. electronic fetal monitoring
    D. pap smear
    E. urine analysis

5. All of the following substances or conditions are harmful to the fetus during gestation EXCEPT   5._____

    A. tetracycline       B. alcohol        C. herpes
    D. rubella            E. thalidomide

6. The use of an intrauterine device (IUD) has been associated with increased risk of   6._____

    A. ectopic pregnancy
    B. pelvic inflammatory disease
    C. infertility
    D. infections
    E. all of the above

7. The number of deaths among infants less than 28 days old per 1,000 live births is called the _____ mortality rate.   7._____

   A. neonatal           B. post-neonatal
   C. fetal              D. perinatal
   E. none of the above

8. All of the following are causes of postneonatal mortality EXCEPT   8._____

   A. lower respiratory tract infections
   B. intrauterine growth retardation
   C. congenital anomalies
   D. sudden infant death syndrome
   E. injuries, e.g., motor vehicle accidents

9. All of the following are important factors in the identification of high risk parents and in the management and prevention of infant health problems EXCEPT   9._____

   A. intrauterine infections
   B. pre-existing maternal illnesses
   C. paternal age
   D. maternal history of reproductive problems
   E. family history of hereditary disease

10. Screening for which of the following conditions has been proven to be cost effective?   10._____

    A. Phenylketonuria       B. Congenital hypothyroidism
    C. Lead poisoning        D. Tuberculosis
    E. All of the above

11. Children _____ are more likely to receive inadequate well-child care.   11._____

    A. with chronic health problems
    B. on medicaid
    C. of mothers who started receiving prenatal care late in the second or third trimester
    D. of parents whose jobs do not provide health insurance
    E. all of the above

12. Injuries are classified by the intent or purposefulness of occurrence. All of the following are classified as intentional injuries EXCEPT   12._____

    A. child abuse           B. motor vehicle mishaps
    C. sexual assault        D. domestic violence
    E. abuse of the elderly

13. Schizophrenia is a disorder, or group of disorders, with a variety of symptoms that include   13._____

    A. delusions             B. hallucinations
    C. agitation             D. apathy
    E. all of the above

14. All of the following are true about the incidence and prevalence of bipolar disorder EXCEPT:   14._____

A. Approximately 4-5% of the population is at risk
B. More women are admitted to the hospital with the diagnosis of bipolar disorder than men
C. The manic form occurs primarily in younger individuals
D. Bipolar patients are more likely to be unmarried
E. The depressive form occurs primarily in older individuals

15. In schizophrenia, there is an increased risk for all of the following EXCEPT

    A. malabsorption syndrome
    B. arteriosclerotic heart disease
    C. hypothyroidism
    D. cancer
    E. none of the above

16. A 6-month-old Jewish infant has a history of seizures, progressive blindness, deafness, and paralysis with an exaggerated startle response to sound.
    The MOST likely diagnosis is

    A. phenylketonuria        B. Gaucher's disease
    C. Tay Sachs disease      D. homocystinuria
    E. maple syrup disease

17. The MOST common inborn error of amino acid metabolism results in

    A. phenylketonuria        B. maple syrup disease
    C. homocystinuria         D. albinism
    E. Gaucher's disease

18. The MOST common lysosomal storage disease is

    A. Niemann-Pick disease   B. Gaucher's disease
    C. Tay Sachs disease      D. homocystinuria
    E. none of the above

19. All of the following are true about spina bifida EXCEPT:

    A. The most common type is spina bifida occulta
    B. The least severe form is myelocoele
    C. Encephalocoele is the rarest type
    D. The most common site affected is lower back
    E. The familial risk of recurrence is approximately 5%

Questions 20-25.

DIRECTIONS: For each metal listed in Questions 20 through 25, select the condition in the column below that is MOST likely to result from chronic exposure to it.

20. Lead
21. Arsenic
22. Cadmium
23. Mercury
24. Beryllium
25. Zinc

A. Osteomalacia-like disease
B. Granulomas of skin and lungs
C. Abnormal sperms
D. Nasal septal ulceration
E. Visual field abnormalities
F. Metal fume fever

# KEY (CORRECT ANSWERS)

| | | | |
|---|---|---|---|
| 1. | D | 11. | E |
| 2. | D | 12. | B |
| 3. | C | 13. | E |
| 4. | C | 14. | D |
| 5. | C | 15. | D |
| 6. | E | 16. | C |
| 7. | A | 17. | A |
| 8. | B | 18. | C |
| 9. | C | 19. | B |
| 10. | E | 20. | C |

21. D
22. A
23. E
24. B
25. F

# EXAMINATION SECTION
# TEST 1

DIRECTIONS: Each question or incomplete statement is followed by several suggested answers or completions. Select the one that BEST answers the question or completes the statement. *PRINT THE LETTER OF THE CORRECT ANSWER IN THE SPACE AT THE RIGHT.*

1. The _____ virus MOST likely causes AIDS.  1.____

    A. picorna
    B. retro
    C. rhino
    D. para influenza
    E. respiratory syncytial

2. Which of the following is MOST likely impaired in patients with HIV?  2.____

    A. Complement
    B. T-cell mediated immunity
    C. B-cell mediated immunity
    D. Basophil
    E. Eosinophil

3. Common modes of transmission of the HIV virus is through  3.____

    A. contaminated needles
    B. transfusion of blood or blood products
    C. intimate sexual contact
    D. infected mother to fetus
    E. all of the above

4. Which of the following vaccines should NOT be given to a child with HIV?  4.____

    A. OPV
    B. Hemophilus type B
    C. MMR
    D. DTP
    E. Pneumococcal

5. All of the following are true statements regarding confidentiality about AIDS EXCEPT:  5.____

    A. No one besides the child's physician has an absolute need to know the child's primary diagnosis.
    B. The family has the right to inform the school.
    C. The teacher has the right to inform other students.
    D. Persons involved in the care and education of an infected student must respect the student's right to privacy.
    E. Confidential records should be maintained.

6. Adults with HIV infection working in a day care center or a school  6.____

    A. should consult their physician regarding the safety of their continuing to work
    B. are not immuno-compromised if they have symptomatic HIV infection
    C. asymptomatic HIV infected adult may care for children in school with skin lesions and open wounds
    D. are at low risk from infectious diseases of children
    E. none of the above

7. A 16-year-old male comes to you for advice about how to protect himself from HIV infection.
   You should tell him all of the following EXCEPT:

   A. Don't inject drugs.
   B. Don't share needles with other people.
   C. Don't have multiple sexual partners.
   D. Use contraceptive pills for sexual contact.
   E. Use condoms for sexual contacts.

8. Among the following, the MOST common cause of focal intracerebral lesions in patients with AIDS is

   A. cryptococcoma
   B. toxoplasmosis
   C. kaposi's sarcoma
   D. mycobacterium tuberculosis abscess
   E. lymphoma

9. A risk factor associated with heterosexual transmission of AIDS includes

   A. lack of condom
   B. anal intercourse
   C. sex during menses
   D. number of sexual contacts
   E. all of the above

10. The MOST frequent malignancy seen in homosexual men with HIV is

    A. kaposi sarcoma
    B. oat cell carcinoma of lung
    C. medullary carcinoma of thyroid
    D. seminoma
    E. infiltrating carcinoma of breast

11. Mother to infant transmission of HIV occurs in approximately _____% of the infants born to seropositive mothers.

    A. 2-5     B. 8-12     C. 15-30     D. 50     E. 75

12. The MOST frequent neurologic clinical manifestation of primary HIV-1 infection includes

    A. peripheral neuropathy
    B. meningoencephalitis
    C. retro orbital pain
    D. cognitive/affective impairment
    E. all of the above

13. The MOST likely dermatologic manifestation of primary HIV-1 infection includes

    A. diffuse urticaria         B. desquamation
    C. alopecia                  D. mucocutaneous ulceration
    E. all of the above

14. Recommendation for the early stages of disease due to HIV infection include

    A. update immunization
    B. no treatment currently is indicated
    C. monitor CD4 every 3 to 6 months
    D. patient education
    E. all of the above

15. An important role of the AIDS counselor is as

    A. teacher
    B. advisor
    C. support person
    D. interviewer
    E. all of the above

16. All of the following are important objectives of HIV test counseling EXCEPT

    A. facilitating client decision-making skills
    B. providing client education about drugs
    C. encouraging responsible client sexual behavior
    D. encouraging and assisting client in making personal changes in their behavior to reduce their risk of re-exposure
    E. assisting the client in developing and modifying risk reduction plans to maintain behavior change

17. The AIDS counselor must help the client deal with all of the following emotional issues EXCEPT

    A. disclosing HIV status to partner
    B. coping with a positive test result
    C. making decisions about having children
    D. making sexual behavior change
    E. encouraging behavior regarding frequent drug use

18. During short-term counseling sessions, communication skills are the most important tools.
    These skills include

    A. culturally sensitive communication
    B. verbal communication skills
    C. reflective listening
    D. all of the above
    E. none of the above

19. The statement regarding verbal counseling skills that is NOT helpful is:

    A. Elicit more information in less time.
    B. Elicit information in more time so as to gain confidence of the patient.
    C. Express respect and honesty.
    D. Often begin with how, what, where, when, and why.
    E. Ask for information or explanations.

20. HIV confidentiality law requires HIV test counselors to discuss

    A. the nature of AIDS
    B. the nature of HIV-related illness
    C. legal protection against AIDS discrimination
    D. behavior known to pose risk for transmission and contraction of HIV infection
    E. all of the above

21. All of the following are non-HIV-related medical complications of substance abuse EXCEPT

    A. lymphoma of brain        B. hepatitis
    C. endocarditis             D. cellulitis
    E. subcutaneous abscesses

22. All of the following statements about HIV/AIDS in women are true EXCEPT:

    A. AIDS has become the number one cause of death for women 20-44 years of age.
    B. AIDS deaths among women have quadrupled in four years.
    C. Women are the fastest growing population with HIV in the United States.
    D. AIDS is one of the five leading causes of death for women.
    E. In New York, AIDS is more common among whites than blacks.

23. The risk factor for female-to-female transmission include

    A. current or former male partner at risk
    B. current or former female partner at risk
    C. history of sharing needles
    D. recipient of artificial insemination
    E. all of the above

24. Clinical manifestations of HIV disease in women include all of the following EXCEPT

    A. chronic vaginal candidiasis
    B. single episode of pharyngitis
    C. cervical dysplasia
    D. frequent outbreak of severe genital herpes
    E. frequent episode of severe PID

25. Recommendations for HIV serologic testing include

    A. persons who have sexually transmitted disease
    B. IV drug users
    C. gay and bisexual men
    D. patients with active tuberculosis
    E. all of the above

# KEY (CORRECT ANSWERS)

| | | | |
|---|---|---|---|
| 1. | B | 11. | C |
| 2. | B | 12. | E |
| 3. | E | 13. | E |
| 4. | A | 14. | E |
| 5. | C | 15. | E |
| 6. | A | 16. | B |
| 7. | D | 17. | E |
| 8. | B | 18. | D |
| 9. | E | 19. | B |
| 10. | A | 20. | E |

21. A
22. E
23. E
24. B
25. E

———

# TEST 2

DIRECTIONS: Each question or incomplete statement is followed by several suggested answers or completions. Select the one that BEST answers the question or completes the statement. *PRINT THE LETTER OF THE CORRECT ANSWER IN THE SPACE AT THE RIGHT.*

1. The HIGHEST seroprevalence rates of HIV in the United States is among

   A. prostitutes
   B. gay men
   C. hemophiliacs who received clotting factor before 1985
   D. IV drug abusers
   E. partners of HIV-infected persons

2. Among the following, the TRUE statement regarding a patient with HIV positive test is:

   A. 80% of patients will die in the first five years.
   B. 30-50% of patients will go on to develop AIDS in 6 years.
   C. A person with positive test without development of AIDS is not considered infectious.
   D. A person with positive test without development of AIDS is not capable of transmitting the infection to others.
   E. None of the above

3. A 24-year-old male has accidental parental exposure (needle stick) to HIV-infected blood.
   The BEST estimate of the risk of HIV infection following such a single parental exposure is one per _____ exposures.

   A. 10      B. 50      C. 100      D. 250      E. 1,000

4. A drug of choice for prophylaxis of a patient exposed to HIV-contaminated needle is

   A. zidoudine              B. stavudine
   C. acyclovir              D. dideoxycytidine
   E. didanosine

5. The prophylaxis should be initiated _____ after exposure.

   A. within one hour and no later than 72 hours
   B. within one week
   C. within one month
   D. within three months
   E. prophylaxis is not required

6. All of the following are true statements regarding prevention of occupational HIV transmission and body substance precautions EXCEPT:

   A. Needles should never be re-capped using both hands.
   B. Gloves should be worn whenever touching mucous membranes or broken skin.
   C. Protective goggles and mask should be avoided if splash exposure is likely.
   D. Gowns should be worn when patient care is expected to soil clothing.
   E. Sharp objects should be deposited into a puncture-proof disposal container as soon as possible.

7. Initial laboratory evaluations of patients with HIV include all of the following EXCEPT

   A. CBC with differential and platelets
   B. base line electrolyte, bun, creatinine, and liver function test
   C. CD4 count, lactate dehydrogenase, and G6-PD
   D. blood culture, urine culture, and CSF culture
   E. VDRL, hepatitis B serologies, and PPD tuberculin test

8. _____ percent of patients with AIDS acquire mai cm-ovium-intracollulare infection in their lifetime.

   A. 100
   B. 25-50
   C. 0-5
   D. 5-10
   E. 75-90

9. The individuals and institutions authorized to receive HIV-related information under the New York State public health law include all of the following EXCEPT:

   A. An authorized foster care or adoption agency
   B. The patient or a person authorized by law who consented to the test on behalf of the patient
   C. A family friend visiting the patient asks you about the diagnosis
   D. Anyone whom the patient has specifically authorized to receive such information by signing a written release
   E. A committee or organization responsible for reviewing or monitoring a health facility

10. When you assist a client in coping with an HIV test result, you should be prepared to deal with the client's emotions including

    A. disbelief
    B. depression
    C. anger
    D. fear of death
    E. all of the above

11. A client with positive HIV test results should be told that

    A. the HIV test shows that antibody to HIV is present
    B. a positive test does not mean he has AIDS or will necessarily develop AIDS
    C. he can infect others with HIV
    D. all of the above
    E. none of the above

12. If the client requests a repeat HIV test to confirm his HIV positive status, you will tell him

    A. HIV test is over 98% accurate for detecting HIV antibody
    B. retesting is not considered necessary but will be provided upon his request
    C. that you expect the HIV retest will be positive
    D. none of the above
    E. all of the above

13. If you are counseling a woman with HIV positive status who recently gave birth to a child, you would tell her all of the following EXCEPT:

    A. Her positive status does not necessarily mean that her baby is infected with HIV.
    B. Only 20 to 30% of babies born to HIV positive mothers get the disease.
    C. The baby will test HIV positive for its whole life.
    D. Her baby will test HIV positive at birth if she has antibodies to HIV.
    E. If the baby is not infected, the baby should test negative by 18 to 24 months of age.

14. Children of biological parents who are HIV positive should be told by the counselor that

    A. they should be tested for HIV
    B. infants may become infected with HIV due to maternal/ child transmission
    C. children born with possible maternal/child transmission should be tested immediately after birth
    D. female partners of HIV positive men should be referred for testing and counseling
    E. all of the above

15. An infant is born to a mother who has antibodies to HIV, and tests positive. At what age should you recommend retesting for HIV?

    A. 2 to 4 months
    B. 6 to 8 months
    C. 10 to 12 months
    D. 18 to 24 months
    E. No retesting required

16. Medical management of HIV positive clients includes

    A. regular medical monitoring
    B. testing of immune system
    C. early treatment in view of weak immune system
    D. all of the above
    E. none of the above

17. A comprehensive medical evaluation of a client suffering from HIV include all of the following EXCEPT

    A. test for immune system
    B. complete medical and personal history
    C. detailed physical exam
    D. testing for sexually transmitted diseases
    E. serial lumbar punctures

18. The immune system of HIV positive clients can be strengthened by all of the following EXCEPT

    A. avoiding alcohol and drug abuse
    B. avoiding stress
    C. blood testing weekly
    D. getting regular exercise
    E. eating a balanced diet

19. In advising clients, it would be IMPROPER to 19._____
    A. include the partner or spouse
    B. exclude family members from the counseling
    C. create support groups
    D. give alcohol or drug treatment
    E. give family planning counseling

20. Partner notification should be effected by all of the following methods EXCEPT: 20._____
    A. Such notification should be done through the patient
    B. Through former sex and needle-sharing partner
    C. In case of inability of the client to disclose, client should be coached
    D. People concerned should be made aware of all programs run by the state
    E. A client should be given a written referral for programs in the area

## KEY (CORRECT ANSWERS)

| | | | |
|---|---|---|---|
| 1. | C | 11. | D |
| 2. | B | 12. | E |
| 3. | D | 13. | C |
| 4. | A | 14. | E |
| 5. | A | 15. | D |
| 6. | C | 16. | D |
| 7. | D | 17. | E |
| 8. | B | 18. | C |
| 9. | C | 19. | B |
| 10. | E | 20. | A |

# EXAMINATION SECTION
## TEST 1

DIRECTIONS: Each question or incomplete statement is followed by several suggested answers or completions. Select the one that BEST answers the question or completes the statement. *PRINT THE LETTER OF THE CORRECT ANSWER IN THE SPACE AT THE RIGHT.*

1. The MOST widely available test to diagnose HIV is

    A. western blot test
    B. T-cell subset
    C. elisa
    D. radioimmunoprecipitation assay
    E. P24 antigen assays

    1.____

2. A 24-year-old male has a positive elisa test for HIV.
   Which of the following would be the NEXT test to confirm this diagnosis?

    A. T-cell subset
    B. P24 antigen assays
    C. Absolute lymphocyte count
    D. Western blot test
    E. Southern blot test

    2.____

3. The drug of choice to treat toxoplasmic encephalitis is

    A. corticosteroids          B. acyclovir
    C. pyrimethamine            D. clindamycin
    E. ampicillin

    3.____

4. All of the following statements are true for preventing toxoplasmosis in patients with HIV EXCEPT:

    A. Wash hands thoroughly after handling raw meat.
    B. Wash fruit and vegetables before consumption.
    C. Avoid contact with material that is potentially contaminated with cat feces.
    D. Avoid touching mucous membranes of mouth and eyes while handling raw meat.
    E. Avoid cooking meat above 30° C.

    4.____

5. All of the following are radiographic manifestations of pulmonary tuberculosis in patients with AIDS EXCEPT

    A. hilar adenopathy
    B. mediastinal adenopathy
    C. apical infiltrates
    D. localized infiltrates limited to middle lobe
    E. localized infiltrates limited to lower lung fields

    5.____

6. Uninfected children born to seropositive mothers may retain passively acquired maternal antibody for

    A. 2 months              B. 4 months
    C. 4-6 months            D. 6-18 months
    E. 2-4 years

    6.____

7. A 25-year-old HIV-infected male has a CD4 count of less than 500 cells per microliter. What therapy should you recommend for this patient?

   A. Sulfadiazine
   B. Dapsone
   C. Corticosteroids
   D. Zidovudine
   E. Zalcitibine

8. Dose-limiting side effects of zidovudine (AZT) include all of the following EXCEPT

   A. hepatitis
   B. glaucoma
   C. neutropenia
   D. thrombocytopenia
   E. toxic myopathy

9. Pneumocystis carinii prophylaxis should be recommended if the patient has _____ CD4 cells per microliter.

   A. a symptomatic disease with 1000
   B. 500
   C. less than 200
   D. 800
   E. none of the above

10. A 25-year-old female with HIV has low-grade fever, drenching night sweats, productive cough with white frothy sputum, and dyspnea of exertion. X-ray study of chest is significant for diffuse perihilar heterogeneous density.
    The MOST likely diagnosis is

    A. acute bacterial endocarditis
    B. pneumocystis carinii pneumonia
    C. congestive heart failure
    D. pulmonary lymphoma
    E. none of the above

11. Which of the following is the MOST sensitive test to diagnose pneumocystis carinii pneumonia?

    A. Chest x-ray
    B. Sputum induction
    C. Broncho-alveolar lavage
    D. Transbronchial biopsy
    E. Gallium scan

12. A 30-year-old patient with known HIV develops severe pneumocystis carinii pneumonia which fails to respond to therapy with TMP/SMX.
    The drug of choice for this patient should be

    A. pentamidine/sethionate
    B. dapsone
    C. prednisone
    D. ceftazidine
    E. pyrimethamine

13. The major side effect of pentamidine therapy may include all of the following EXCEPT

    A. hypotension
    B. ventricular tachycardia
    C. hypercalcemia
    D. acute pancreatitis
    E. hyperkalemia

14. Among the following, the MOST likely organism to cause CNS mass lesion in a patient    14._____
    with AIDS is

    A. mycobacterium tuberculosis
    B. cryptocococcus newformans
    C. coccidioides immitis
    D. toxoplasma gondii
    E. Candida albican

15. What is the treatment of choice for the patient in the previous question?    15._____

    A. Pyrimethamine           B. Primaquine
    C. Amphotericine           D. Fluconazole
    E. Isoniazid

16. Methemoglobinemia is the MOST common side effect of    16._____

    A. primaquine              B. dapsone
    C. clindamycin             D. trimethoprim
    E. zidovudine

17. A 34-year-old female with known HIV comes to see you with complaints of blurred vision,    17._____
    decreased visual acuity, and the presence of floaters. Opthalmological examination
    reveals creamy yellowish-white granular areas with perivascular exudates and hemor-
    rhage (cotton wool spots).
    The MOST likely causative organism for this is

    A. herpes simplex          B. cryptococcal neoformans
    C. toxoplasma gondii       D. treponema pallidum
    E. cytomegalovirus

18. The MOST likely treatment for the patient in the previous question is    18._____

    A. ganciclovir             B. amphotericine
    C. pyrimethamine           D. penicillin
    E. foscarnet

19. A 32-year-old white male who has had pneumocystis pneumonia in the past comes in for    19._____
    a routine evaluation.
    On physical examination, you note a violaceous palpable firm nodule on the back of
    the neck 1-1.5 cm. in diameter.
    What procedure should you perform NEXT?

    A. Antibiotic therapy      B. Simple excision
    C. Corticosteroid therapy  D. Biopsy of lesion
    E. Vincristin

20. What is the MOST likely diagnosis of the patient's condition in the previous question?    20._____

    A. Keloid                  B. Granuloma
    C. Kaposi sarcoma          D. Melanoma
    E. Basal cell carcinoma

21. What is the treatment of choice in an HIV patient with widespread symptomatic kaposi's sarcoma?

    A. Observation only
    B. Zidovudine
    C. Radiotherapy
    D. Doxorubicin
    E. Cryotherapy

22. Anal neoplasia in an HIV patient is MOST frequently associated with

    A. herpes virus
    B. parvo virus
    C. human papiloma virus
    D. Epstein-Barr virus
    E. cryptosporidium

23. Among the following, the MAJOR differential diagnosis of HIV infection includes

    A. Epstein-Barr virus mononucleosis
    B. cytomegalovirus mononucleosis
    C. viral hepatitis
    D. secondary syphilis
    E. all of the above

24. A person with _____ should have tuberculin skin testing.

    A. HIV
    B. positive tuberculin skin test 6 months ago
    C. abnormal chest roentgenograms compatible with past tuberculosis
    D. recent contacts of persons known to have, or suspected of having, clinically active tuberculosis
    E. cough, hemophysis, weight loss

25. A tuberculin reaction of 5 mm. or more is classified as positive in persons

    A. with known or suspected HIV infection
    B. who have chest radiographs with fibrotic lesion likely to represent old, healed tuberculosis
    C. who have had close recent contact with a patient with infectious tuberculosis
    D. all of the above
    E. none of the above

# KEY (CORRECT ANSWERS)

| | | | |
|---|---|---|---|
| 1. | C | 11. | D |
| 2. | D | 12. | A |
| 3. | C | 13. | C |
| 4. | E | 14. | D |
| 5. | C | 15. | A |
| 6. | D | 16. | B |
| 7. | D | 17. | E |
| 8. | B | 18. | A |
| 9. | C | 19. | D |
| 10. | B | 20. | C |

21. D
22. C
23. E
24. B
25. D

# TEST 2

DIRECTIONS: Each question or incomplete statement is followed by several suggested answers or completions. Select the one that BEST answers the question or completes the statement. *PRINT THE LETTER OF THE CORRECT ANSWER IN THE SPACE AT THE RIGHT.*

1. A 30-year-old male is recently diagnosed as having HIV infection. The initial guidelines for antiretroviral therapy in this patient includes:

    A. If he does not have any symptoms and CD4 count at 500 or above, continue observation and clinical and immunological monitoring every six months
    B. If there are no symptoms and CD4 count between 200 and 500 and patient remains stable, initiate anti-retroviral therapy
    C. If symptomatic, and CD4 count is between 200 and 500, begin antiretroviral therapy
    D. All of the above
    E. None of the above

2. Indication for PCP prophylaxis in an adult patient with HIV includes all of the following EXCEPT

    A. CD4 count less than 200/mm$^3$
    B. CD4 count less than 20% of total lymphocytes
    C. CD4 count more than 500/mm$^3$
    D. symptomatic HIV infection
    E. history of prior pneumocystis carinii pneumonia CPCD

3. Indication for pneumocystis carinii pneumonia (PCP) prophylaxis in children includes

    A. infected infants are less than 15 months of age
    B. children 15 to 24 months have CD4 count less than 750/mm$^3$ or less than 20% of total lymphocytes
    C. children 24 months to 6 years have CD4 count less than 500/mm$^3$ or less than 20% of total lymphocytes
    D. seropositive infants less than 12 months have CD4 count less than 1500/mm$^3$
    E. all of the above

4. A 7-year-old male with HIV infection is recently diagnosed having pulmonary tuberculosis for which he was placed on multiple drug regimen. Now he is having red-green vision discrimination.
The drug MOST likely causing this problem is

    A. rifampin          B. ethambutol
    C. pyrazinamide      D. isoniazid
    E. streptomycin

5. An absolute contraindication for zidovudine therapy is

    A. if patient does not return for follow-up
    B. breastfeeding
    C. WBC less than 1000/mm$^3$ or absolute neutrophil count less than 500/mm$^3$
    D. pregnancy
    E. hemoglobin concentration of 78 gm/dl

6. At what age should you start referring a child with HIV to the dentist?

   A. One year
   B. Two years
   C. Three years
   D. Five years
   E. Ten years

7. Multidrug resistant tuberculosis is MORE common in patients who

   A. had prior antituberculous drug therapy
   B. had a history of intravenous substance use
   C. are homeless
   D. have a history of incarceration
   E. all of the above

8. Unless the pattern of susceptibility is known, which of the following drug combinations is recommended to treat tuberculosis in HIV patients?

   A. Isoniazid plus rifampin
   B. Pyrazinamide plus ethambutol
   C. Iosoniazid plus rifampin plus pyrazinamide plus ethambutol
   D. Isoniazid plus pyrazinamide
   E. Isoniazid plus ethambutol

9. Which of the following statements is NOT true about monitoring isoniazid drug toxicity?

   A. Base line liver function test should not be performed in all patients before initiating INH therapy.
   B. INH should be discontinued when liver function enzyme exceeds 3 to 5 times that of base line.
   C. Liver function test should be repeated if there are clinical signs of liver disease.
   D. Liver function should be performed more frequently in patients with underlying liver disease.
   E. Liver function test should be performed more frequently in asymptomatic patients with elevated baseline values.

10. All of the following statements are true regarding rifampin EXCEPT:

    A. Rifampin may cause standard doses of oral contraceptives to be ineffective.
    B. Rifampin interacts with methadone, requiring increased methadone dosages.
    C. Rifampin interacts with methadone requiring decreased methadone dosages.
    D. Rifampin turns urine, tears, and other body fluids orange.
    E. Single drug therapy with rifampin is not effective to treat tuberculosis in HIV patients.

11. Which of the following is NOT a cause of false-negative EIA reaction to HIV-1?

    A. Bone marrow transplantation
    B. Stevens-Johnson syndrome
    C. B cell dysfunction
    D. Incubation period of acute disease before seroconversion
    E. Intensive or long-term immune suppressive therapy

12. The causes of false positive EIA reactions to HIV-1 includes all of the following EXCEPT    12.___
    A. chronic renal failure
    B. HIV-2 infection
    C. severe alcoholic liver disease
    D. replacement transfusion
    E. sclerosing cholangitis

13. A 24-year-old female with AIDS develops intolerance to zidovudine (AZT) therapy.    13.___
    Among the following, the drug of choice for this patient is
    A. didanosine (DDI)          B. acyclovir
    C. zalcitabine               D. ribavirin
    E. suramin

14. The predominant immunologic defect in acquired immune deficiency syndrome is a    14.___
    quantitative and qualitative defect of
    A. B-lymphocytes             B. complement system
    C. helper T-cell             D. suppressor T-cell
    E. none of the above

15. The MOST common finding in a child with HIV infection is    15.___
    A. non-Hodgkin's lymphoma    B. Kaposi sarcoma
    C. recurrent otitis media    D. brain abscesses
    E. gout

Questions 16-21

DIRECTIONS: Match the conditions in Questions 16 through 21 with the appropriate drug therapy in Column I.

### COLUMN I

A. Clarithromycin
B. Amphotericin
C. Trimethoprim and sulfamethoazole
D. Foscarne
E. Pyrimethamine
F. Erythromycin

16. Isospora                         16.___

17. Aspergillosis                    17.___

18. M. ovium-intracellulare          18.___

19. Cytomagalovirus retinitis        19.___

20. Toxoplasma encephalitis          20.___

21. Rochaumaea quintana              21.___

Questions 22-26.

DIRECTIONS: Match the conditions in Questions 22 through 26 with the relevant symptom in Column I.

## COLUMN I

- A. Brain imaging evidence of a lesion having a mass effect
- B. A violaceous plaque-like lesion on skin or mucus membrane
- C. Discrete patches of retinal whitening with a distinct border spreading in a centrifugal manner
- D. Recent onset of retrosteral pain on swallowing
- E. Arterial blood gas analysis showing arterial $PO_2$ of less than 70 mmHg

22. Candidiasis of esophagus     22._____

23. Cytomegalovirus     23._____

24. Kaposi sarcoma     24._____

25. Toxoplasmosis     25._____

26. Pneumocystis carinii     26._____

Questions 27-30.

DIRECTIONS: Match the drug inhibitors in Questions 27 through 30 with the sites of possible antiviral activity in Column I.

## COLUMN I

- A. Uncoating of virus
- B. Attachment and penetration
- C. Translation and assembly
- D. Transcription by reverse transcriptase of HIV

27. Zidovudine     27._____

28. Interferon     28._____

29. Peptide T     29._____

30. Glycoslation inhibitors     30._____

## KEY (CORRECT ANSWERS)

| | | | | |
|---|---|---|---|---|
| 1. | D | | 16. | C |
| 2. | C | | 17. | B |
| 3. | E | | 18. | A |
| 4. | B | | 19. | D |
| 5. | C | | 20. | E |
| 6. | C | | 21. | B |
| 7. | E | | 22. | D |
| 8. | C | | 23. | C |
| 9. | A | | 24. | B |
| 10. | C | | 25. | A |
| 11. | B | | 26. | E |
| 12. | D | | 27. | D |
| 13. | A | | 28. | A |
| 14. | C | | 29. | B |
| 15. | C | | 30. | C |

# EXAMINATION SECTION
# TEST 1

DIRECTIONS: Each question or incomplete statement is followed by several suggested answers or completions. Select the one that BEST answers the question or completes the statement. *PRINT THE LETTER OF THE CORRECT ANSWER IN THE SPACE AT THE RIGHT.*

Questions 1-4.

DIRECTIONS: Questions 1 through 4 are to be answered on the basis of the following information.

A 45-year-old patient is admitted with a severe frontal headache. After a thorough examination, meningitis is ruled out. A CT scan of the head shows multiple ring enhancing lesions. His $CO_4$ count is 54, and western blot test is positive for HIV.

1. The MOST likely diagnosis of this condition is

    A. cytomegalovirus
    B. mycobacterium aviam intracellulare
    C. histoplasmosis
    D. toxoplasmosis

2. The nurse should do all of the following to protect herself from AIDS infection EXCEPT

    A. exercise care when handling sharp instruments
    B. use disposable mouthpieces and airways instead of direct mouth to mouth resuscitation
    C. wash gloves before use with another patient
    D. wash hands after removing gloves and between patient contact

3. To improve the nutritional status of the patient, all of the following measures should be adopted EXCEPT

    A. including patient in decision-making process regarding his nutritional care
    B. try to give drugs before meals
    C. encourage patient to maximize nutritional intake during periods when he is feeling better
    D. discourage excessive alcohol intake, which has an immunosuppressive effect

4. Nursing interventions facilitating patient understanding of the goals of therapy and methods to prevent HIV transmission include

    A. encouraging patient to discuss feelings and concerns about the plan of therapy and changes in work, home, and lifestyle environment
    B. using a nonjudgmental approach during care
    C. warning patient not to share toilet articles or donate blood or organs
    D. all of the above

Questions 5-8.

DIRECTIONS: Questions 5 through 8 are to be answered on the basis of the following information.

A 29-year-old black male has a cough with mucopurulent sputum, hemoptysis, and dyspnea, with a history of low-grade fever, night sweats, and weight loss. His laboratory workup confirms the diagnosis of pulmonary tuberculosis.

5. Risk factors for the activation of tuberculosis include all of the following EXCEPT    5.___

    A. close contact with someone who has infectious tuberculosis
    B. infection with a sexually transmitted disease
    C. a tuberculin skin test which has recently converted to a significant reaction
    D. declining immunity or infection with HIV

6. Nursing education of this patient would NOT include    6.___

    A. techniques to control propagation of secretions while coughing
    B. stressing the need to breathe only filtered, humidified air
    C. stressing the importance of a nutritious diet
    D. all of the above

7. In a preventive treatment plan for tuberculosis, isoniazid prophylaxis should be offered to all of the following EXCEPT    7.___

    A. household members and other close associates of potentially infectious tuberculous cases
    B. persons recently testing negative to tuberculin reaction
    C. newly infected persons
    D. persons with past tuberculosis

8. Complications of isoniazid therapy that a nurse should have in mind when initiating prophylaxis include all of the following EXCEPT    8.___

    A. persistent paresthesias of the hands and feet
    B. progressive liver damage
    C. loss of appetite, fatigue, joint pain, and dark urine
    D. bone marrow suppression

9. Nursing guidelines for the prevention of salmonella infections do NOT include    9.___

    A. washing hands after using the toilet, particularly during illness and carrier states
    B. raw eggs or egg drinks should not be ingested
    C. purchase only kosher meats and meat products
    D. all food from animal sources should be thoroughly cooked

10. After eating lunch in a roadside restaurant, a patient develops fever, crampy abdominal pain, diarrhea, mixed blood and mucus, and profound prostration.    10.___
    Nursing interventions in the management of this disorder include all of the following EXCEPT

    A. assessing patient for dehydration
    B. offering a caffeinated liquid during acute stage of illness
    C. assisting in epidemiological study of every patient in whom organism is found
    D. instructing patient to avoid taking antimotility agents

11. Measures which should be taken in the prevention of this disorder do NOT include   11.____

   A. prophylactic vaccination of all children under 12 years of age
   B. a program of fly control
   C. surveillance of water sanitation
   D. an adequate sewage disposal program

Questions 12-13.

DIRECTIONS:   Questions 12 and 13 are to be answered on the basis of the following information.

After drinking water from a restaurant, a 25-year-old man develops fever, headache, malaise, a non-productive cough, and irregularly spaced small rose-colored spots on his abdomen, chest, and back. His pulse is relatively slow in comparison with his fever.

12. All of the following complications may be expected in this patient EXCEPT   12.____

   A. intestinal hemorrhage and perforation
   B. thrombophelibitis
   C. multiple sclerosis
   D. osteomyelitis

13. Environmental hygiene should be established to prevent enteric fever in endemic areas by   13.____

   A. avoiding all fresh fruits and vegetables
   B. homogenization of all milk and dairy products
   C. protection and purification of water supplies
   D. all of the above

Questions 14-16.

DIRECTIONS:   Questions 14 through 16 are to be answered on the basis of the following information.

Two days after a 29-year-old male was hit by a car, he develops headache, fever, and becomes hyperirritable and restless, with rigidity of both flexor and extensor muscles. After a thorough laboratory investigation, he is diagnosed with a case of tetanus.

14. Complications that may be expected in this patient include all of the following EXCEPT   14.____

   A. dysrhythmias          B. cerebrovascular accident
   C. cardiac arrest        D. bacterial shock

15. Nursing interventions in preventing respiratory and cardiovascular complications include all of the following EXCEPT   15.____

   A. monitoring for dysphagia
   B. providing cardiac monitoring
   C. delaying intubation and mechanical ventilation as long as possible if spasms are interfering with respiratory function
   D. maintaining an adequate airway

16. Nursing interventions in the ongoing assessment and support of this patient include

    A. placing the patient in a completely dark, soundproof environment to avoid stimulating reflex spasms
    B. watching for excessive urinary output
    C. avoiding sudden stimuli and light as the slightest stimulation may trigger paroxysmal spasms
    D. all of the above

17. Lyme disease is caused by borrelia burgdorferi and is introduced by an ixodid tick. Nursing instructions for people living in or visiting an endemic area would NOT include

    A. applying insect repellent
    B. tucking pants into boots or socks
    C. removing tick with forceps, exerting slow, steady upward pull, and avoid squeezing the tick
    D. cut a shallow X across the tick bite with a sterile blade

18. Nursing interventions to make patients aware of sexual practices that will reduce the chances of acquiring a sexually transmitted disease include all of the following EXCEPT

    A. avoiding sex with individuals who have had multiple partners
    B. not using water-soluble lubricants
    C. avoiding douching before and after sex
    D. use latex condoms lubricated with nonoxynol-9

19. Diseases that are NOT transmitted via respiratory secretions include

    A. tuberculosis
    B. AIDS
    C. rubeola
    D. rheumatic fever

20. Diseases transmitted via blood and body fluids do NOT include

    A. AIDS
    B. hepatitis B
    C. hepatitis A
    D. all of the above

21. Patients at high risk for social isolation include those infected with

    A. tetanus
    B. tuberculosis
    C. AIDS
    D. all of the above

22. All of the following conditions are prevalent in advanced age EXCEPT

    A. osteoporosis
    B. scoliosis
    C. cataracts
    D. multiple sclerosis

23. Impaired physical mobility related to muscular weakness may be found in patients with

    A. Parkinson's disease
    B. rheumatoid arthritis
    C. cerebral palsy
    D. all of the above

24. Nursing interventions to assist patients in coping with their health problems do NOT include

    A. referral to support groups
    B. understanding and patience
    C. referral for psychoanalysis
    D. none of the above

25. Patients with, conditions that may be expected to degenerate include those with

    A. cerebrovascular accidents
    B. multiple sclerosis
    C. spinal cord injuries
    D. all of the above

## KEY (CORRECT ANSWERS)

| | | | |
|---|---|---|---|
| 1. | D | 11. | A |
| 2. | C | 12. | C |
| 3. | B | 13. | C |
| 4. | D | 14. | B |
| 5. | B | 15. | C |
| 6. | B | 16. | C |
| 7. | B | 17. | D |
| 8. | D | 18. | B |
| 9. | C | 19. | B |
| 10. | B | 20. | C |

| | |
|---|---|
| 21. | D |
| 22. | D |
| 23. | A |
| 24. | C |
| 25. | B |

# TEST 2

DIRECTIONS: Each question or incomplete statement is followed by several suggested answers or completions. Select the one that BEST answers the question or completes the statement. *PRINT THE LETTER OF THE CORRECT ANSWER IN THE SPACE AT THE RIGHT.*

Questions 1-6.

DIRECTIONS: Questions 1 through 6 are to be answered on the basis of the following information.

A 29-year-old white male has a closed, oblique fracture of the tibia and fibula resulting from a traffic accident.

1. Nursing interventions in the management of this patient involve all of the following EXCEPT

    A. relieving pain and discomfort
    B. promoting complete physical immobilization
    C. preventing the development of disuse syndrome
    D. promoting a positive psychological response to trauma

2. In the above patient, a closed reduction is done and a cast is applied. Nursing interventions to dry a plaster cast properly include all of the following EXCEPT

    A. avoid handling cast when wet, if possible; handle with palms, not fingertips
    B. avoid placing the cast on a hard surface while drying
    C. use a heat lamp or hair dryer to speed drying time
    D. not to completely cover the cast

3. Nursing care of the patient to maintain good circulation after the cast is applied does NOT include

    A. observing for the five P's (pain, pallor, paralysis, paresthesia, and pulselessness) of neurovascular assessment for muscle ischemia
    B. observing circulatory status in exposed fingers or toes
    C. cutting out pressure areas of the cast on the extremity
    D. all of the above

4. In this type of fracture, complications associated with immobility include all of the following EXCEPT

    A. loss of muscle strength and endurance
    B. loss of range of motion/joint contracture
    C. pressure sores at bony prominences
    D. muscular hypertrophy

5. Nursing interventions to aid in preventing development of thromboembolism include

    A. encourage immobility, do not change position frequently, and discourage ambulation
    B. elevate legs to prevent statis, avoiding pressure on blood vessels

C. avoid elastic stockings or sequential compression devices
D. all of the above

6. In setting the discharge plan, the nurse should advise the patient to

   A. adjust usual lifestyle and responsibilities to accommodate limitations imposed by fracture
   B. start active exercises and continue with isometric exercises after the cast is removed
   C. carefully limit the amount of weight bearing that will be permitted on the fractured extremity
   D. all of the above

Questions 7-9.

DIRECTIONS: Questions 7 through 9 are to be answered on the basis of the following information.

A 65-year-old female suffers a fracture of the right hip joint after slipping on a wet floor. After thorough evaluation of the case, a total hip replacement is performed.

7. Nursing interventions in promoting the comfort of the patient include all of the following EXCEPT

   A. placing a pillow on the outer sides of both the legs to keep affected leg in adduction
   B. with two nurses positioned on each side of the bed, using the draw sheet to lift and reposition the patient in bed
   C. placing the patient in a supine position, placing a pillow under the affected leg from mid-thigh to ankle, keeping the leg in a neutral rotation
   D. handling the affected extremity gently

8. All of the following complications may be suspected in this patient EXCEPT

   A. pneumonia            B. cardiac arrest
   C. fat emboli           D. infection

9. In discussing the discharge plan with the patient and her family, the nurse should recommend all of the following precautions EXCEPT:

   A. Do not lift heavy objects
   B. Do not cross or twist legs
   C. Observe carefully for signs of wound infection
   D. Try to sleep on operative side

10. A 20-year-old male has a suspected fracture of the lumbar spine.
    Nursing interventions to avoid complications associated with spinal fracture and immobility do NOT include

    A. measures to prevent risk of thromboembolism complications
    B. monitoring bowel and bladder function
    C. encouraging the patient to ambulate as soon as possible
    D. all of the above

11. Traction is the force applied in a specific direction. Purposes of traction include all of the following EXCEPT

    A. reduction and immobilization of the fracture
    B. increasing muscle spasms
    C. regaining normal length and alignment of an injured extremity
    D. preventing deformity

12. Nursing interventions in the care of a patient on traction do NOT include

    A. encouraging deep breathing hourly to facilitate expansion of lungs and movement of respiratory secretions
    B. encouraging active exercise of uninvolved muscles
    C. adding progressively heavier weights to the traction apparatus
    D. that the traction must be continuous to be effective

13. Total hip replacement is indicated in all of the following clinical conditions EXCEPT

    A. complete dislocation of the hip joint
    B. pathological fractures from metastatic cancer
    C. femoral neck fracture
    D. congenital hip disease

14. A 26-year-old male has an above knee amputation performed after severe traumatic injury.
    Nursing intervention in the education of this patient includes teaching

    A. the patient and his family how to wrap the residual limb with elastic bandage to control edema and to form a firm conical shape for prosthesis fitting
    B. the patient residual limb-conditioning by pushing the residual limb against a soft pillow
    C. methods of care of the residual limb and prosthesis, washing and drying the limb thoroughly at least twice a day, and removing all soap residue to prevent skin irritation or infection
    D. all of the above

15. A patient with multiple myeloma is admitted to the hospital.
    Nursing interventions to prevent pathological fractures include

    A. assisting the patient in movement with gentleness and patience
    B. allowing the joints to bend freely when repositioning the patient
    C. keeping the patient immobile
    D. all of the above

16. A 58-year-old nulliparous white female is admitted for alcohol detoxification. In the assessment of this patient, the nurse notes that she is at high risk for osteoporosis. The nurse should advise the patient all of the following EXCEPT

    A. dietary supplements to minimize bone mass
    B. participating in dietary education related to vitamin D intake
    C. vigorous exercise
    D. strategies to prevent falls

17. A 38-year-old patient is admitted for rheumatoid arthritis. Nursing interventions to aid the patient in adjusting to the chronic nature of this condition include all of the following EXCEPT

    A. advising that continuous immobilization may decrease pain
    B. allowing the patient to express fears and concerns
    C. encouraging continued follow-up to re-evaluate progression of disease and efficacy of drug therapy
    D. teaching the patient to avoid sudden jarring movements of joints

18. Predisposing factors for a herniated lumbar disk include all of the following EXCEPT

    A. sedentary occupations
    B. frequent physical exercise
    C. long-term driving, e.g., truckdriver
    D. participation in bowling or baseball

19. Nursing interventions to keep a patient with a herniated lumbar disk free of pain include

    A. bed rest on a firm mattress with bed board; traction as ordered
    B. administering morphine every 6-8 hours
    C. encouraging an exercise program of trunk-twists and deep knee bends
    D. all of the above

20. Indications for surgical intervention in patients with herniated lumbar disks include all of the following EXCEPT

    A. prevention of further nerve damage and deficits
    B. intermittent back and leg pain
    C. sensory and motor deficits in lower extremities
    D. bowel and bladder dysfunction

Questions 21-23.

DIRECTIONS: Questions 21 through 23 are to be answered on the basis of the following information.

A 25-year-old male sustains an acute head injury after a traffic accident.

21. Nursing interventions for the detection of CSF or blood draining from the nose or ears include all of the following EXCEPT

    A. observe and record, at least hourly, any leak of blood or clear fluid from the nose or ears
    B. pack nose or ears
    C. immediately report to physician if any drainage is found
    D. drain fluid onto sterile towels or dressings

22. Nursing interventions to keep the patient free from infection or injury include

    A. seizure precautions
    B. strict aseptic techniques during all invasive procedures
    C. restricting visitors with any respiratory illness
    D. all of the above

23. The patient is undergoing intracranial surgery.
    Nursing interventions to prevent post-operative complications include all of the following EXCEPT

    A. checking ears, nose, and dressings for drainage
    B. suctioning through the nose
    C. supporting head when turning the patient
    D. monitoring breathing, advising the patient that he must not cough

24. A 75-year-old woman is admitted with CVA caused by hemorrhage.
    Nursing interventions in the care of this patient include all of the following EXCEPT

    A. elevating head of the bed 30-45° to improve venous drainage
    B. decreasing environmental stimuli
    C. turning patient gently to the affected side
    D. maintaining complete bedrest until bleeding has been controlled and patient's condition is stable

25. In a patient with Parkinson's disease, nursing interventions to help maintain gastrointestinal integrity include all of the following EXCEPT

    A. providing adequate fluid intake
    B. restricting carbohydrates
    C. providing a high-fiber diet
    D. administering stool softeners or laxatives as ordered

26. Nursing interventions to maintain positive body image and self-concept would NOT include

    A. providing clothes that are simple to put on
    B. supervising and assisting in skin care and personal hygiene
    C. installing a mirror that can easily be seen by the patient
    D. all of the above

27. Myasthenia gravis is diagnosed in a 45-year-old white female.
    Nursing interventions to keep the patient free from respiratory impairment include which of the following?

    A. Postural drainage; turning patient frequently
    B. Diaphragmatic breathing exercises to maintain strength with maximum ventilation and minimum energy expenditure
    C. Balancing physical activities with rest
    D. All of the above

28. Nursing care to keep the patient mentioned above well-nourished would NOT include

    A. providing small, frequent, semisolid or fluid meals that are nutritious and high in potassium
    B. inserting a feeding tube
    C. observing for aspiration; keeping suction equipment available
    D. allowing patient to eat meals without rushing

Questions 29-30.

DIRECTIONS: Questions 29 and 30 are to be answered on the basis of the following information.

A 30-year-old white female develops nystagmus, intentional tremors, and spastic weakness of limbs. She also has a history of sudden falls while standing, dropping things out of her hands, and urinary incontinence. After a thorough diagnostic work-up, she is diagnosed with multiple sclerosis.

29. Nursing interventions in this case do NOT include

    A. encouraging optimal activity level
    B. promoting adequate rest periods to prevent exhaustion
    C. providing self-help devices for eating, ambulation, and reading
    D. restraining patient while in bed

30. Nursing interventions to make the patient clearly under stand and express her fears do NOT include

    A. talking to the patient and family together and separately
    B. encouraging patient to begin psychotherapy treatment
    C. allowing expression of depression and hopelessness
    D. clarifying misconceptions and lack of information about present status and prognosis

# KEY (CORRECT ANSWERS)

| | | | |
|---|---|---|---|
| 1. | B | 11. | B |
| 2. | C | 12. | C |
| 3. | C | 13. | A |
| 4. | D | 14. | D |
| 5. | B | 15. | A |
| 6. | D | 16. | A |
| 7. | A | 17. | A |
| 8. | B | 18. | B |
| 9. | D | 19. | A |
| 10. | C | 20. | B |
| 21. | B | 26. | C |
| 22. | D | 27. | D |
| 23. | B | 28. | B |
| 24. | C | 29. | D |
| 25. | B | 30. | B |

# EXAMINATION SECTION
# TEST 1

DIRECTIONS: Each question or incomplete statement is followed by several suggested answers or completions. Select the one that BEST answers the question or completes the statement. *PRINT THE LETTER OF THE CORRECT ANSWER IN THE SPACE AT THE RIGHT.*

1. The purpose of treating Parkinson's disease with Levodopa is to    1.____

    A. increase the production of acetylcholine
    B. replace dopamine in the brain cells
    C. improve the myelination of the neurons of the basal ganglia
    D. regenerate the neurons of the basal ganglia

2. Which of the following is NOT a possible major side effect of tetracyclines?    2.____

    A. Impaired kidney function
    B. Bone defects (in small children)
    C. Phototoxicity
    D. Neurotoxicity

3. Which of the following drugs may be prescribed for the prevention and treatment of gout?    3.____

    A. Acetominophen         B. Hydrocortisone
    C. Colchicine            D. Ibuprofen

4. A client with tetanus should be observed closely for    4.____

    A. pallor and perspiration
    B. respiratory spasms
    C. muscled rigidity
    D. involuntary muscle spasms

5. Vomiting should NOT be induced for poisonings involving    5.____

    A. acetaminophen         B. petroleum distillates
    C. plant parts           D. salicylate

6. After a spinal cord injury, a client should be encouraged to drink fluids in order to    6.____

    A. prevent meningal infections
    B. avoid gangrene
    C. prevent urinary tract infections
    D. balance fluids and electrolytes

7. A nurse should use a tilt table in treating an arthritic client in order to    7.____

    A. prevent pressure ulcers
    B. prevent calcium loss
    C. promote spinal hyperextension
    D. prevent muscular atrophy

8. For an unimmunized 14-month-old, initial immunizations would include each of the following EXCEPT

   A. oral poliovirus vaccine
   B. DTP
   C. Td
   D. tuberculin test

9. Which lobe of the cerebral cortex is responsible for registering general sensations of heat, cold, pain, and touch?

   A. Occipital  B. Parietal  C. Temporal  D. Frontal

10. A client is admitted to the emergency room with a sucking stab wound on the right side of the thorax. Into what position should the nurse place the client?

    A. On the back, with the head elevated
    B. In a high-Fowler's position with the right side supported
    C. On the left side, flat, with a pillow supporting the left arm
    D. On the right side, with the head elevated

11. The FIRST symptom of open-angle glaucoma is

    A. persistent headaches
    B. continually blurred vision
    C. uncontrollable twitching of the eye
    D. impaired peripheral vision

12. Respiratory isolation would be recommended for a client with

    A. cholera
    B. diphtheria
    C. laryngeal tuberculosis
    D. meningitis

13. The diet for a client being treated for ulcerative colitis may include each of the following EXCEPT

    A. raw bran
    B. milk
    C. hot cereal
    D. sliced apple

14. Which of the following is a common early symptom of myasthenia gravis?

    A. Blurred vision
    B. Double vision
    C. Migraine headaches
    D. Tearing

15. A client taking ampicillin at home should notify the physician

    A. if diarrhea develops
    B. when symptoms disappear entirely
    C. when a negative culture is obtained
    D. if drowsiness occurs

16. If a client experiences a generalized motor seizure, the nurse's primary responsibility is to

    A. insert a plastic airway between the teeth
    B. restrain the client's movements for safety
    C. clear the immediate environment for safety
    D. administer the prescribed anticonvulsant

17. For what purpose are clients encouraged to perform deep breathing exercises following surgery?   17.____

    A. Increasing cardiac output
    B. Expanding residual volume
    C. Increasing blood volume
    D. Counteracting respiratory acidosis

18. Which of the following would be experienced by a client with multiple sclerosis?   18.____

    A. Tremors                B. Double vision
    C. Mental confusion       D. Respiratory congestion

19. To reduce the risk of toxoplasmosis, pregnant women should be taught to avoid   19.____

    A. cleaning the cat box
    B. unprotected sex
    C. stagnant pools of water
    D. eating marine animals

20. For a client who has just undergone an above-the-knee amputation, the nurse should work to avoid a hip contracture by   20.____

    A. making sure the client lies in the prone position several times a day
    B. making sure the client sits in a chair frequently throughout the day
    C. propping the stump with pillows
    D. elevating the head of the client's bed

21. Following the repair of an inguinal hernia, the nurse can BEST help the recovering client by   21.____

    A. applying an abdominal binder
    B. encouraging frequent coughing
    C. placing a rolled towel under the scrotum
    D. encouraging a high-carbohydrate diet

22. Which of the following would MOST likely be discovered during a nursing assessment of a client with Meniere's disease?   22.____

    A. Hypotension
    B. Diplopia
    C. Hearing loss
    D. Jerky lateral eye movement

23. Due to concern for the development of blackwater fever, a client with malaria should be closely observed for   23.____

    A. dark red urine        B. low-grade fever
    C. vomiting              D. nausea

24. Which of the following substances is released by axons supplying skeletal muscles?   24.____

    A. Potassium             B. Acetylcholine
    C. ATP                   D. Epinephrine

25. Which of the following is NOT considered to be an antimicrobial secretion of the human body?  25.___

    A. Tears
    C. Mucus
    B. Gastric juice
    D. Vaginal secretions

---

# KEY (CORRECT ANSWERS)

1. B
2. D
3. B
4. B
5. B

6. C
7. B
8. C
9. C
10. D

11. D
12. D
13. B
14. B
15. A

16. C
17. D
18. B
19. A
20. A

21. C
22. D
23. A
24. B
25. C

---

# TEST 2

DIRECTIONS: Each question or incomplete statement is followed by several suggested answers or completions. Select the one that BEST answers the question or completes the statement. *PRINT THE LETTER OF THE CORRECT ANSWER IN THE SPACE AT THE RIGHT.*

1. Which of the following is the MOST likely cause of osteoporosis? 1.____

    A. Iron deficiency
    B. Prolonged inactivity
    C. Prolonged period of low WBC
    D. Estrogen therapy

2. Which of the following is an early sign of lead poisoning in children? 2.____

    A. Mental confusion       B. Anemia
    C. Tremors                D. Yellow sclerae

3. If a client's mouth appears pulled to the right, it is an indication of injury to the _____ nerve. 3.____

    A. left vestibular        B. left trigeminal
    C. right abducent         D. right facial

4. Which of the following medications would NOT be used to treat gangrene? 4.____

    A. Tetracycline           B. Chloramphenicol
    C. Streptomycin sulfate   D. Penicillin G

5. Which of the following would be experienced by a client with tic dolourex, or trigeminal neuralgia? 5.____

    A. Yellow sclerae
    B. Uncontrollable twitching of eyelid
    C. Unilateral muscle paralysis
    D. Extreme head and facial pain

6. Following a laminectomy, which of the following is the primary postoperative complication that should be observed for? 6.____

    A. Cerebral edema
    B. Compression of spinal cord
    C. Bladder spasms
    D. Increased intracranial pressure

7. Each of the following results from a streptococci infection that enters via the upper respiratory tract EXCEPT 7.____

    A. mononucleosis          B. puerperal sepsis
    C. rheumatic fever        D. shigellosis

8. After being admitted to the emergency room for injuries sustained in a serious automobile accident, a client undergoes a splenectomy. In the immediate postoperative period, the nurse should watch for 8.____

A. intestinal bleeding or obstruction
B. peritonitis
C. hemorrhage or distended abdomen
D. infection or shock

9. What type of stool should be expected from a client that has a colostomy on the left side of the abdomen?

    A. Coated with stringy mucus
    B. Bloody
    C. Moist and formed
    D. Liquid

10. In bites involving the lower extremities, the incubation period for rabies is about

    A. 10 days      B. 40 days      C. 2 months      D. 4 months

11. Clients with spinal cord injuries sometimes experience sympathetic hyperreflexia. Each of the following is a sign or symptom of this condition EXCEPT

    A. pulsating headache          B. goose bumps
    C. pallor                      D. diaphoresis

12. Which of the following positions would be appropriate for a client suffering from cerebral thrombosis?

    A. Semi-Fowler's               B. Sims'
    C. Trendlenburg                D. Prone

13. A diagnosis of *thrush* actually refers to a(n)

    A. acid-fast bacterial infection
    B. protozoan parasite
    C. virus
    D. yeast infection

14. Osteoarthritis is MOST likely to involve the joints of the

    A. metacarpals and fingers     B. knees and hips
    C. shoulders and elbows        D. metatarsals and ankles

15. Which of the following laboratory tests would be helpful in confirming a diagnosis of systemic lupus erythematosus?

    A. WBC                         B. Blood pH
    C. Blood gases                 D. BUN

16. Which of the following is NOT a therapeutic intervention involved in the treatment of tetanus?

    A. Penicillin G
    B. Diazepam to limit spasms
    C. Cleansing of would with aqueous benzalkonium chloride
    D. Wound debridement to allow exposure to air

17. A client experiencing left hemiplagia following a cerebral vascular accident would suffer paralysis of each of the following EXCEPT the

    A. left arm
    B. left eyelid
    C. left leg
    D. right side of the face

18. Which of the following, observed in a client, would indicate malaria?

    A. Erythrocytosis
    B. Leukocytosis
    C. Splenomegaly
    D. Increased sedimentation rate

19. Which of the following side effects may be a consequence of treating cerebral edema with dexamethasone?

    A. Involuntary muscle contracture
    B. Hypotension
    C. Increased intracranial pressure
    D. Hyperglycemia

20. *Full-thickness* burns are so classified because they have extended to involve damage to the

    A. epidermis
    B. upper dermis
    C. subcutaneous layer
    D. muscular tissue

21. The MAJOR problem encountered by newly paraplegic clients is

    A. atrophy
    B. control of the bladder
    C. ambulation
    D. formation of urinary calculi

22. When the spinal cord is crushed above the level of the phrenic nerve origin, _____ will result.

    A. respiratory paralysis
    B. vagus nerve dysfunction
    C. cardiac arrhythmia
    D. retention of sensation in lower extremities

23. An adolescent epileptic client who has been taking Dilantin develops status epilepticus. The MOST likely reason for this is that the

    A. prescribed dosage of Dilantin was insufficient for the client's activity level
    B. client failed to take the prescribed dosage consistently
    C. client has built up a tolerance for the prescribed dosage
    D. seizures are becoming more intense in response to the prescribed dosage

24. The test that is performed immediately to confirm a diagnosis of meningitis is 24.____

    A. blood culture  
    B. lumbar puncture  
    C. meningomyelogram  
    D. alkaline phosphatase

25. Which of the following is the relay center for sensory impulses? 25.____

    A. Thalamus  
    B. Cerebellum  
    C. Medulla oblongata  
    D. Pons

## KEY (CORRECT ANSWERS)

| | | | |
|---|---|---|---|
| 1. B | | 11. C | |
| 2. B | | 12. B | |
| 3. D | | 13. D | |
| 4. C | | 14. B | |
| 5. D | | 15. D | |
| 6. B | | 16. C | |
| 7. D | | 17. B | |
| 8. C | | 18. C | |
| 9. C | | 19. D | |
| 10. D | | 20. C | |

21. B  
22. A  
23. B  
24. B  
25. A

# TEST 3

DIRECTIONS: Each question or incomplete statement is followed by several suggested answers or completions. Select the one that BEST answers the question or completes the statement. *PRINT THE LETTER OF THE CORRECT ANSWER IN THE SPACE AT THE RIGHT.*

1. What type of antibiotics operate by blocking tRNA attachment to cell ribosomes?  1.____

    A. Tetracyclines  
    B. Erythromycins  
    C. Cephalosporins  
    D. Penicillins

2. The primary goal of the medical treatment of chronic glaucoma is  2.____

    A. preventing secondary infections
    B. pupil dilation
    C. increasing ocular range of motion
    D. the control of intraocular pressure

3. A client with a peptic ulcer would be permitted to eat or drink each of the following EXCEPT  3.____

    A. milk  
    B. oatmeal  
    C. applesauce  
    D. orange juice

4. After a fracture of the hip, what is/are the MOST frequently developed contracture(s)?  4.____

    A. Flexion and adduction of the hip
    B. Hyperextension of the knee
    C. External rotation
    D. Internal rotation

5. Which of the following clinical findings would NOT support a diagnosis of Crohn's disease?  5.____

    A. Occult blood in stool
    B. Anemia
    C. Elevated WBC
    D. Severe pain in right lower quadrant

6. Which of the following produce antibodies?  6.____

    A. Erythrocytes  
    B. Plasma cells  
    C. Eosiniphils  
    D. Lymphocytes

7. Which of the following is NOT a common cause of gastritis?  7.____

    A. Chronic uremia
    B. Allergic reactions
    C. Zollinger-Ellison syndrome
    D. Bacterial or viral infection

8. When administering chloramphenicol to an infected client, a nurse should  8.____

    A. observe for anticoagulant effect
    B. observe for neuromuscular blockage

C. assess blood work before and during therapy
D. be watchful for false positive urine tests

9. A client with rheumatoid arthritis should be taught to

   A. maintain the limbs in a position of extension
   B. place pillows beneath the knees
   C. remain in a semi-Fowler's position as long as possible
   D. assume positions that are most comfortable

10. A client, who was earlier admitted with multiple serious injuries sustained in an accident, is diagnosed with a stress ulcer. The nurse should watch for, and immediately report,

    A. nausea and headache
    B. diaphoresis and cold extremities
    C. diarrhea and distention
    D. warm, flushed skin and complaints of thirst

11. Because of the behavior of damaged cells, clients with serious burns should have levels of _____ checked frequently.

    A. vitamin A            B. sodium
    C. potassium            D. calcium

12. Injury or infection of the _____ nerve is MOST likely to be the cause of nerve deafness.

    A. facial               B. trigeminal
    C. cochlear             D. vestibular

13. Each of the following is a symptom of severe cinchonism EXCEPT

    A. deafness             B. blood in the urine
    C. severe nausea        D. vertigo

14. The irreversible effects of untreated lead poisoning are imposed mainly upon the _____ system.

    A. lymphatic            B. digestive
    C. urinary              D. central nervous

15. Which of the following signs would indicate developing thrombophlebitis following pelvic surgery?

    A. Edematous ankles
    B. A painful, tender area on the leg
    C. A reddened area at ankle and knee joints
    D. Pruritis on the thigh

16. Which of the following would increase a client's risk of osteoporosis?

    A. A history of hyperparathyroidism
    B. Long-term steroid therapy
    C. Excessive estrogen consumption
    D. Frequent strenuous physical activity

17. What is the term for an internal antimicrobial protein agent that destroys certain gram-negative bacteria and viruses?

    A. Properdin
    B. Lysozyme
    C. Amantadine
    D. Interferon

18. Nerve fibers that are destroyed in the brain or spinal cord do not regenerate because they do not have

    A. nuclei
    B. a sodium pump
    C. a neurilemma
    D. a myelin sheath

19. Which crutch gait should be taught to a client fitted with a prosthesis after a single leg amputation?

    A. Three-point
    B. Four-point
    C. Swing-through
    D. Tripod

20. After surgery of the biliary tract, clients are at risk for developing respiratory infections because

    A. bile in the blood causes lowered resistance
    B. pathogens are transferred from bile to the blood
    C. the incision is adjacent to the diaphragm
    D. the anesthesia involved in lengthy surgery weakens immunity

21. When assessing a client suspected for increased intra-cranial pressure, the nurse may expect to discover any of the following EXCEPT

    A. rapid pulse rate
    B. psychotic behavior
    C. nausea or vomiting
    D. impaired pupil reactivity

22. When an organism enters a wound and produces a toxin which causes crepitus, what disease has been produced?

    A. Salmonella
    B. Botulism
    C. Gas gangrene
    D. Tetanus

23. Which of the following laboratory tests should a nurse refer to in order to aid in the diagnosis of arthritis?

    A. Creatinine level
    B. Bence Jones protein
    C. Antinuclear antibody
    D. Sodium level

24. Which of the following is a characteristic manifestation of rabies?

    A. Confusion or memory loss
    B. Pharyngeal spasm
    C. Echolalia
    D. Diarrhea

25. Which of the following assessment findings would NOT support a diagnosis of hiatal hernia?

    A. Nocturnal dyspnea
    B. Regurgitation
    C. Respiratory pain
    D. Heartburn after eating

## KEY (CORRECT ANSWERS)

1. A
2. D
3. D
4. A
5. A

6. B
7. C
8. C
9. A
10. D

11. C
12. C
13. B
14. D
15. B

16. B
17. A
18. C
19. B
20. C

21. A
22. C
23. C
24. B
25. C

---

# TEST 4

DIRECTIONS: Each question or incomplete statement is followed by several suggested answers or completions. Select the one that BEST answers the question or completes the statement. *PRINT THE LETTER OF THE CORRECT ANSWER IN THE SPACE AT THE RIGHT.*

1. Which of the following is considered to be the MOST common complication of peptic ulcer?

    A. Varices of the esophagus
    B. Perforation
    C. Hemorrhage
    D. Pyloric stenosis

    1.____

2. A client is admitted to the emergency room following a serious automobile accident in which she suffered head injuries. Soon after admission, her temperature is measured at 102.6°F.
   This suggests an injury to the

    A. pons Varolii            B. optic chiasm
    C. temporal lobe           D. hypothalamus

    2.____

3. Which of the following side effects may be experienced by a client taking sulfonamides for treatment of a urinary tract infection?

    A. Diarrhea                B. Fatigue
    C. Photosensitivity        D. Nephrotoxicity

    3.____

4. A client suffering from myasthenia gravis would receive a dosage of neostigmine in order to

    A. accelerate neural transmission
    B. block the action of cholinesterase
    C. stimulate the cerebral cortex
    D. boost immunity

    4.____

5. When tetracycline is given orally, it should be given

    A. an hour before milk or dairy products are ingested
    B. with a meal or snack
    C. with an antacid
    D. with orange juice or other citrus juice

    5.____

6. 48 hours after a cerebral vascular accident, the client should begin

    A. exercises designed to actively return muscle function
    B. isometric exercises
    C. active exercises of all extremities
    D. passive range-of-motion exercises

    6.____

7. Following surgery, a client's feedings are administered by nasogastric tube. Shortly after the feedings begin, the client develops diarrhea.
   Which of the following is a possible solution?

    7.____

A. Decreasing the carbohydrate content of the formula
B. Decreasing the protein content of the formula
C. Diluting the formula with water
D. Switching to IV feedings

8. Which of the following is a common side effect associated with Dilantin?

   A. Facial tics
   B. Impaired pupil response
   C. Tinnitus
   D. Hypertrophy of the gums

9. Contact isolation would be imposed on a client with each of the following infections EXCEPT

   A. impetigo
   B. chickenpox
   C. herpes simplex
   D. acute respiratory infections in children

10. A client with an ileostomy would normally present a stool that is

    A. solid and clay-colored
    B. flecked with blood
    C. liquid
    D. pencil-shaped

11. When caring for a child with acute laryngitis, the nurse's main concern should be

    A. reduction of fever
    B. constant delivery of 40% humidified oxygen
    C. increased fluid intake
    D. constant respiratory monitoring

12. Which of the following medications is used to treat tic dolourex, or trigeminal neuralgia?

    A. Morphine sulfate
    B. Carbamazepine
    C. Halol
    D. Allopurinol

13. A client who suffered a spinal cord injury three weeks earlier suffers from coffee-ground emesis and restlessness. The nurse should

    A. check hemoglobin levels in laboratory reports
    B. insert a nasogastric tube
    C. change the client to a liquid diet
    D. check for occult blood in the stool

14. Following a splenectomy, a client should be observed carefully for the depletion of

    A. vitamin A
    B. potassium
    C. calcium
    D. sodium

15. A nurse could expect each of the following clinical findings from a client with Lyme disease EXCEPT

    A. swollen joints
    B. enlarged spleen
    C. lack of coordination
    D. paralysis

16. By what route do meningitis-producing bacteria enter the central nervous system? 16.____

    A. Sinuses
    B. Pores
    C. Gastrointestinal tract
    D. Urinary tract

17. Which of the following results from a Group A beta-hemolytic streptococcal infection? 17.____

    A. Mononucleosis
    B. Rheumatic fever
    C. Rheumatoid arthritis
    D. Hepatitis A

18. Which of the following drugs is MOST commonly used to treat rheumatoid arthritis? 18.____

    A. Gold salts
    B. Hydrocortisone
    C. Aspirin
    D. Ibuprofen

19. Worsening colitis is often treated by placing the patient on a bland, residue-free diet and by administering vitamins parenterally. The purpose of this treatment is to 19.____

    A. increase intestinal absorption
    B. reduce gastric acidity
    C. minimize colonic irritation
    D. boost electrolytes

20. Stump shrinkage following an amputation is caused by muscular atrophy and 20.____

    A. subcutaneous fat reduction
    B. postoperative edema
    C. loss of bone tissue
    D. skin turgor

21. During a client's early post-burn phase, the nurse's PRIMARY objective should be to 21.____

    A. restore fluid volume
    B. initiate tissue repair
    C. relieve pain
    D. prevent infection

22. Which of the following would NOT typically be part of a nursing care plan for a client with systemic lupus erythematosus? 22.____

    A. Dosages of vitamin C
    B. Renal dialysis
    C. Administration of corticosteroids
    D. Avoiding exposure to sunlight

23. Which of the following is a serious complication of acute malaria? 23.____

    A. Fluid and electrolyte imbalance
    B. Lung congestion
    C. Seizure of peristalsis
    D. Anemia

24. Gold salts used to treat rhematoid arthritis involve the serious side effect of 24.____

    A. emboli
    B. gastric pain
    C. decreased cardiac output
    D. kidney damage

25. Which of the following is NOT a gram-negative, rod-shaped bacteria?   25._____

    A. Shigella
    C. Escherichia
    B. Neisseria
    D. Salmonella

---

## KEY (CORRECT ANSWERS)

1. C
2. D
3. C
4. B
5. A

6. D
7. A
8. D
9. B
10. C

11. D
12. B
13. A
14. B
15. B

16. A
17. B
18. C
19. C
20. A

21. A
22. B
23. A
24. D
25. B

---

# EXAMINATION SECTION

## TEST 1

DIRECTIONS: Each question or incomplete statement is followed by several suggested answers or completions. Select the one that BEST answers the question or completes the statement. *PRINT THE LETTER OF THE CORRECT ANSWER IN THE SPACE AT THE RIGHT.*

1. The one of the following which is the BEST description of a properly objective investigator is one who
   A. is friendly and sensitive to the client's feelings, without becoming emotionally involved
   B. is distant and impersonal, remaining unaffected by what the client says
   C. lets personal emotions enter as far as the client's situation calls for them
   D. becomes emotionally involved with the client's situation but without showing involvement

   1._____

2. The one of the following which is MOST necessary for successfully interviewing a person who belongs to a culture different from that of the investigator is for the investigator to
   A. have some appreciation of the other culture
   B. ignore those cultural differences which lead to bias
   C. stay away from sensitive, touchy issues
   D. assume the mannerisms of people in the other culture

   2._____

3. In fact-finding interviews, it is generally assumed that the smaller the number of interviewees, the greater the increase of reliability with the addition of others. The PROPER number of interviewees need to insure the accuracy of information obtain generally depends upon the
   A. educational level of those interviewed
   B. number of people who have the required information
   C. directness of the questions asked
   D. variability of the information received

   3._____

4. The one of the following which is generally MOST likely to be accurately described in an interview by an interviewee is
   A. the presence of a large painting in the investigator's office
   B. the number of people in the investigator's waiting room
   C. space relations
   D. duration of time

   4._____

5. The one of the following which is generally the BEST course of action for an investigator to take when interviewing a person who is reluctant to tell what he knows about a matter under investigation is to
   A. be curt and abrupt, and threaten the person with the consequences of his withholding information

   5._____

B. be firm and severe, and pressure the person into telling the needed information
C. be patient and candid with the person being questioned about the investigation since doing otherwise is not ethical
D. give the person false information about the investigation so he will give the needed information without realizing its importance

6. It is often recommended that an investigator prepare in advance a list of questions or topics to be covered in an interview.
The MAIN reason for such a checklist is to
   A. allow investigations to be assigned to less efficient investigators
   B. eliminate a large amount of follow-up paperwork
   C. aid the investigator in remembering to cover all important documents
   D. aid the investigator in maintaining an objective distance from the person interviewed

7. Usually, the CHIEF advantage of a directive approach in an interview is that the
   A. investigator maintains control over the course of the interview
   B. person interviewed is more likely to be put at ease
   C. person interviewed is generally left free to direct the interview
   D. investigator will not suggest answers to the person interviewed

8. Usually, the CHIEF advantage of a non-directive approach by an investigator in conducting an interview is that the
   A. investigator generally conceals what he is looking for in the interview
   B. person interviewed is more likely to express his true feelings about the topic under discussion
   C. person interviewed is more likely to follow an idea introduced by the investigator
   D. investigator can keep the discussion limited to topics he believes to be relevant

9. The one of the following which is generally the LEAST likely to be accurate in a description of an event given to an investigator is a statement about
   A. the presence of an object
   B. the number of people, when their number is small
   C. locations of people
   D. duration of time

10. Assume that you, an investigator, are conducting a character investigation. In an interview, the one of the following character traits of the person being interviewed which can USUALLY be determined with a good degree of reliability is
    A. honesty           B. dependability
    C. forcefulness      D. perseverance

11. As an investigator, you have been assigned the task of obtaining a family's social history.
The BEST place for you to interview members of the family while obtaining this social history would generally be in
    A. the family's home
    B. your agency's general offices
    C. the home of a friend of the family
    D. your own private office

12. You, an investigator, are checking someone's work history.
The way for you to get the MOST reliable information from a previous employer is to
    A. send personal letters; the employer will respond to the personal attention
    B. send form letters; the employer will cooperate readily since little time or effort is asked of him
    C. arrange a personal interview; the employer may offer information he would not care to put in a letter or speak over the phone
    D. telephone; this method is as effective as a personal interview and is much more convenient

13. The effect that attestation, or the formal taking of an oath, has on witness testimony is to
    A. decrease accuracy, since a witness under oath is more nervous about what is said
    B. makes little difference, since the witness is not too swayed by an oath
    C. increase accuracy, since a witness under oath feels more responsibility for what is said
    D. eliminate inaccuracy unless there is deliberate perjury on the part of the witness

14. If an investigator obtains testimony from persons in interviews by means of interrogation or asking questions rather than by letting the person freely relate the testimony, what is said will GENERALLY be
    A. greater in range and less accurate
    B. greater in range and more accurate
    C. about the same in range and less accurate
    D. about the same in range and more accurate

15. Experienced investigators have learned to phrase their questions carefully in order to obtain the desired response.
Of the following, the question which would usually elicit the MOST accurate answer is:
    A. "How old are you?"
    B. "What is your income?"
    C. "How are you today?"
    D. "What is your date of birth?"

16. The one of the following questions which would generally lead to the LEAST reliable answer is:
    A. "Did you see a wallet?"
    B. "Was the German Shepherd gray?"
    C. "Didn't you see the stop sign?"
    D. "Did you see the guard on duty?"

17. Some investigators may make a practice of observing details of the surroundings when interviewing in someone's home or office.
Such a practice is GENERALLY considered
    A. *undesirable*, mainly because such snooping is unwarranted, unethical invasion of privacy
    B. *undesirable*, mainly because useful information is rarely, if ever, gained this way
    C. *desirable*, mainly because useful insights into the character of the person interviewed may be gained
    D. *desirable*, mainly because it is impossible to evaluate a person adequately without such observation of his environment

18. The one of the following questions which MOST often lead to a reliable answer is:
    A. "Was his hair very dark?"
    B. "Wasn't there a clock on the wall?"
    C. "Was the automobile white or gray?"
    D. "Did you see a motorcycle?"

19. The one of the following which can MOST accurately be determined by an investigator by means of interviewing is
    A. a person's intelligence
    B. factual information about an event
    C. a person's aptitude for a specific task
    D. a person's perceptions of his own abilities

20. The one of the following which is MOST likely to help a person being interviewed feel at ease is for the investigator to
    A. let him start the conversation
    B. give him an abundance of time
    C. be relaxed himself
    D. open the interview by telling a joke

21. If the interviewee is to perceive some goal for himself in the interview and thus be motivated to participate in it, it is important that he clearly understands some of the aspects of the interview.
Of the following aspects, the one the interviewee needs LEAST to understand is
    A. the purpose of the interview
    B. the mechanics of interviewing
    C. the use made of the information he contributes
    D. what will be expected of him in the interview

22. As an investigator working on a project requiring inter-agency cooperation, you find that employees of an agency involved in the project are constantly making it difficult for you to obtain necessary information.
Of the following, the BEST action for you to take FIRST is to
    A. discuss the problem with your supervisor
    B. speak with your counterpart in the other agency

C. discuss the problem with the head of the uncooperative agency
D. contact the head of your agency

23. The investigator is justified in misleading the interviewee only when, in the investigator's judgment, this is clearly required by the problem being investigated.
Such a practice is
   A. *necessary*; there are times when complete honesty will impede a successful investigation
   B. *unnecessary*; such a tactic is unethical and should never be employed
   C. *necessary*; an investigator must be guided by success rather than ethical considerations in an investigation
   D. *unnecessary*; it is clearly doubtful whether such a practice will help the investigator conclude the investigation successfully

23.____

24. Assume that, in investigating a case of possible welfare fraud, it becomes necessary to hold an interview in the client's home in order to observe family interaction and conditions. Upon arriving, the investigator finds that the client's living room is noisy and crowded, with neighbors present and children running in and out.
Of the following, the BEST course of action for the investigator to take is to
   A. conduct the interview in the living room after telling the children to behave and asking the neighbors to leave
   B. tell the client that it is impossible to conduct the interview in the apartment and make an appointment for the next day in the investigators office
   C. suggest that they move from the living room into the kitchen where there is a table on which he can write
   D. try his best to conduct the interview in the noisy and crowded living room

24.____

25. You, an investigator, are giving testimony in court about a matter you have investigated. An attorney is questioning you in an abrasive, badgering way and, in an insulting manner, calls into doubt your ability as an investigator. You lose your temper and respond angrily, telling the attorney to stop harassing and insulting you.
Of the following, the BEST description of such a response is that it is generally
   A. *appropriate*; as a witness in court, you do not have to take insults from anybody, including an attorney
   B. *inappropriate*; losing your temper will show that you are weak and cannot be trusted as an investigator
   C. *appropriate*; a judge and jury will usually respect someone who responds strongly to unjust provocation
   D. *inappropriate*; such conduct is unprofessional and may unfavorably impress a judge and jury

25.____

## KEY (CORRECT ANSWERS)

| | | | |
|---|---|---|---|
| 1. | A | 11. | A |
| 2. | A | 12. | C |
| 3. | D | 13. | C |
| 4. | A | 14. | A |
| 5. | C | 15. | D |
| 6. | C | 16. | B |
| 7. | A | 17. | C |
| 8. | B | 18. | D |
| 9. | D | 19. | D |
| 10. | C | 20. | C |

| | |
|---|---|
| 21. | B |
| 22. | A |
| 23. | A |
| 24. | C |
| 25. | D |

# TEST 2

DIRECTIONS: Each question or incomplete statement is followed by several suggested answers or completions. Select the one that BEST answers the question or completes the statement. *PRINT THE LETTER OF THE CORRECT ANSWER IN THE SPACE AT THE RIGHT.*

1. An investigator may have problems in obtaining information from persons who have a history of mental disturbance CHIEFLY because such persons are
   A. usually highly unstable so that they cannot give a coherent account of anything they have experienced
   B. usually very withdrawn so that they generally are unwilling to talk to anyone they do not know well
   C. often normal in manner so that an investigator may be unaware that their condition may bias information they provide
   D. often violent and may try to attack an investigator who questions them intensively about a topic which is sensitive

    1.____

2. Empathy can be defined as the ability of one individual to respond sensitively and imaginatively to another's feelings.
   For an investigator to be empathetic during an interview is USUALLY
   A. *undesirable*, mainly because an investigator should never be influenced by the feelings of the one being interviewed
   B. *desirable*, mainly because an interview will not be productive unless the investigator takes the side of the person interviewed
   C. *undesirable*, mainly because empathy usually leads an investigator to be biased in favor of the person being interviewed
   D. *desirable*, mainly because this ability allows the investigator to direct his questions more effectively to the person interviewed

    2.____

3. Assume that an investigator must, in the course of an investigation, question several people who know each other.
   To gather them all in one group and question them together is GENERALLY
   A. *good practice*, since any inaccurate information offered by one person would be corrected by others in the group
   B. *poor practice*, since people in a group rarely pay adequate attention to questions
   C. *good practice*, since the investigator will save much time and effort in this way
   D. *poor practice*, since the presence of several people can inhibit an individual from speaking

    3.____

4. While conducting a character investigation of a potential employee, you, as an investigator, notice that most community members interviewed have negative opinions of the candidate.
   Of the following statements about the usefulness of community opinions in such a matter, the one which is LEAST accurate is that

    4.____

83

A. prudence should be exercised in evaluating information received in a community contact
B. a community investigation sometimes elicits gossip which may present an exaggerated picture
C. community opinion is reliable when used to assess an individual's character
D. opinions which cannot be supported by facts must be considered as such

5. An effective investigator should know that the one of the following which LEAST describes why there is a wide range of individual behavior in human relations is that
   A. socio-economic status influences human behavior
   B. physical characteristics do not influence human behavior
   C. education influences human behavior
   D. childhood experience influences human behavior

6. In your investigative unit, you discern a growing friction between two co-workers which is beginning to impede the work of the unit.
   Of the following, the approach you should FIRST adopt is to
   A. mediate the friction yourself; if unsuccessful, then inform your supervisor
   B. ignore the friction; although detrimental, it is beyond your authority to settle
   C. promptly discuss the friction and possible course of action with other members of your unit
   D. promptly inform your supervisor of the friction and let him handle the matter

7. In certain cases, in order that an investigation be conducted successfully, an investigator must have the cooperation of people in the community.
   The one of the following which BEST describes how an investigator may gain community cooperation in an investigation is by
   A. using persuasion
   B. using authority
   C. spending many hours in the community
   D. being friendly with community leaders

8. During a field investigation, an investigator encounters an uncooperative interviewee.
   Of the following, the FIRST thing the investigator should do in such a situation is to
   A. try various appeals to win the interviewee over to a cooperative attitude
   B. try to ascertain the reason for non-cooperation
   C. promise the interviewee that all data will be kept confidential
   D. alter his interviewing technique with the uncooperative interviewee

9. You, as an investigator, discover that an interviewee who was requested to bring with him specific documents for his initial employment interview has forgotten the documents.

Of the following, the BEST course of action to take is to
- A. give the person a reasonable amount of time to furnish the document
- B. tell the person you will let him know how much additional time he could receive
- C. mark the person disqualified for employment; he has failed to provide reasonably requested data on time
- D. mark the person provisionally qualified for employment; upon receipt of the documents, he will be permanently qualified

10. As an investigator checking interviewees' work experience, you realize that the person whom you are to interview is only marginally fluent in English and has, therefore, requested permission to bring a translator with him.
Of the following, the BEST course of action is to inform the interviewee that
    - A. outside translators may not be used
    - B. only city translators may be used
    - C. state law requires fluency in English of all civil servants
    - D. he may be assisted in the interview by his translator

11. Assume that during the course of an interview, an investigator is verbally attacked by the person being interview.
Of the following, it would be MOST advisable for the investigator to
    - A. answer back in a matter-of-fact manner
    - B. ask the person to apologize and discontinue the interview
    - C. ignore the attack but adjourn the interview to another day
    - D. use restraint and continue the interview

12. Assume that an investigator finds that the person he is interviewing has difficulty finishing his sentences and seems to be groping for words.
In such a case, the BEST approach for the investigator to take is to
    - A. say what he thinks the person has in mind
    - B. proceed patiently without calling attention to the problem
    - C. ask the person why he finds it difficult to finish his sentence
    - D. interrupt the interview until the person feels more relaxed

13. The one of the following which BEST describes the effect of the sympathetic approach in interviewing on the interviewee is that it will
    - A. have no discernible effect on the interviewee
    - B. calm the interviewee
    - C. lead the interviewee to understate his problems
    - D. mislead the interviewee

14. The one of the following characteristics which is a PRIMARY requisite for a successful investigative interview is
    - A. total curiosity
    - B. total sympathy
    - C. complete attention
    - D. complete dedication

15. Assume that you, an investigator, become aware that one of your colleagues has a drinking problem which is affecting the operations of your unit.
    Of the following, the action which you should take FIRST is to
    A. give your colleague time to resolve the problem himself
    B. discuss the problem with your colleague
    C. inform your supervisor of the problem
    D. not involve yourself in your colleague's problem

16. Assume that an Assistant District Attorney has asked you, the investigator of an alleged welfare fraud, to conduct a follow-up interview with a primary state witness.
    The one of the following which is MOST important in arranging such an interview is to
    A. keep the witness cooperative
    B. conduct the matter in secret
    C. allow the witness to determine where and when the interview takes place
    D. conduct the interview as soon as possible to insure a strong case

17. Assume that an investigative unit has received a complex task requiring team work.
    Of the following, the one which is LEAST essential to the operations of a team effort is
    A. a small group
    B. a leader
    C. regular interaction between team members
    D. separate office space for each team member

18. By examining a candidate's employment record, an investigator can determine many things about the candidate.
    Of the following, the one which is LEAST apparent from an employment record is the candidate's
    A. character
    B. willingness to work
    C. capacity to get along with co-workers
    D. potential for advancing in civil service

19. Assume that you, an investigator, are conducting an investigative interview in which the person being interviewed is using the interview as a forum for venting his anti-civil service feelings.
    Of the following, the FIRST thing that you should do is to
    A. agree with the person; perhaps that will shorten the outburst
    B. respectfully disagree with the person; the decorum of the interview has already been disrupted
    C. courteously and objectively direct the interview to the relevant issue
    D. reschedule the interview to another mutually agreeable time

20. The pattern of an investigative interview is LARGELY set by the
    A. person being interviewed
    B. person conducting the interview
    C. nature of the investigation
    D. policy of the agency employing the interviewer

    20.____

21. Assume that a person being interviewed, who had been talking freely, suddenly tries to change the subject.
    To a trained interviewer, this behavior would mean that the person PROBABLY
    A. knew very little about the subject
    B. realized that he was telling too much
    C. decided that his privacy was being violated
    D. realized that he was becoming confused

    21.____

22. Assume that you, an investigator, receive a telephone call from an unknown individual requesting information about a case you are currently investigating.
    In such a situation, the BEST course of action for you to take is to
    A. give him the information over the telephone
    B. tell him to write to your department for the information
    C. send him the information, retaining a copy for your files
    D. tell him to call back, giving you additional time to check into the matter

    22.____

23. Assume that you, an investigator, are responding to a written query from a member of the public protesting a certain procedure employed by your agency.
    In such a case, your response should stress MOST the
    A. difficulty that a large agency encounters in trying to treat all members of the public fairly
    B. idea that the procedure in question will be discontinued if enough complaints are received
    C. necessity for the procedure
    D. origin of the procedure

    23.____

Questions 24-25.

DIRECTIONS: Questions 24 and 25 are to be answered in the light of the information given in the following passage.

Assume that a certain agency is having a problem at one of its work locations because a sizable portion of the staff at that location is regularly tardy in reporting to work. The management of the agency is primarily concerned about eliminating the problem and is not yet too concerned about taking any disciplinary action. You are an investigator working for this agency, and though you have never had any contact with this location, you are assigned to investigate to determine, if possible, what might be causing this problem.

After several interviews, you see that low morale created by poor supervision at this location is at least part of the problem. Then, the last person you will interview before submitting your report tells you, when asked the reason for his tardiness, "*Well, I don't know; I just can't get up in the morning. So when I do get going, I've got to rush to get here. And just between you and me, I've lost interest in the job. Working conditions are bad, and it's hard for me to be enthusiastic about working here."*

24. Given the goals of the investigation and assuming that the investor was using a non-directive approach in this interview, of the following, the investigator's MOST effective response should be:
    A. "You know, you are building a bad record of tardiness."
    B. "Can you tell me more about this situation?"
    C. "What kind of person is your superior?"
    D. "Do you think you are acting fairly towards the agency by being late so often?"

24.____

25. Given the goals of the investigation and assuming the investigator was using a directed approach in this interview, of the following, the investigator's response should be
    A. "That doesn't seem like much of an excuse to me."
    B. "What do you mean by saying that you've lost interest?"
    C. What problems are there with the supervision you are getting?"
    D. "How do you think your tardiness looks in your personnel record?"

25.____

## KEY (CORRECT ANSWERS)

| | | | | |
|---|---|---|---|---|
| 1. | C | | 11. | D |
| 2. | D | | 12. | B |
| 3. | D | | 13. | B |
| 4. | C | | 14. | C |
| 5. | B | | 15. | C |
| 6. | D | | 16. | A |
| 7. | A | | 17. | D |
| 8. | B | | 18. | D |
| 9. | A | | 19. | C |
| 10. | D | | 20. | B |

21. B
22. B
23. C
24. B
25. C

# EXAMINATION SECTION

## TEST 1

DIRECTIONS: Each question or incomplete statement is followed by several suggested answers or completions. Select the one that BEST answers the question or completes the statement. *PRINT THE LETTER OF THE CORRECT ANSWER IN THE SPACE AT THE RIGHT.*

1. An investigator uses Forms A, B, and C in filling out his investigation reports. He uses Form B five times as often as Form A, and he uses Form C three times as often as Form B.
   If the total number of all forms used by the investigator in a month equal 735, how many times was Form B used?
   A. 150   B. 175   C. 205   D. 235

   1.____

2. Of all the investigators in one agency, 25% work in a particular building. Of these, 12% have desks on the 14$^{th}$ floor.
   What percentage of the investigators work in this building but do NOT have desks on the 14$^{th}$ floor?
   A. 12%   B. 13%   C. 22%   D. 23%

   2.____

3. An investigator is given two reports to read. Report P is 160 pages long and takes the investigator 3 hours and 20 minutes to read.
   If Report S is 254 pages long and the investigator reads it at the same rate as he reads Report P, how long will it take him to read Report S? _____ hours _____ minutes.
   A. 4; 15   B. 4; 50   C. 5; 10   D. 5; 30

   3.____

4. A team of 6 investigators was assigned to interview 234 people.
   If half the investigators conduct twice as many interviews as the other half, and the slow group interviews 12 persons a day, how many days would it take to complete this assignment? _____ days.
   A. 4½   B. 5   C. 6   D. 6½

   4.____

5. The investigators in one agency conduct an average of 12 interviews an hour from 10 A.M. to 12 noon and from 1 P.M. to 5 P.M. daily. The director of his agency knows from past experience that 20% of those called in to be interviewed are unable to keep the appointments that were scheduled.
   If the director wants his staff to be kept occupied with interviews for the entire time period that has been set aside for this function, how many appointments should be scheduled for each day?
   A. 86   B. 90   C. 96   D. 101

   5.____

6. An investigator has a 430-page report to read. The first day, he is able to read 20 pages. The second day, he reads 10 pages more than the first day, and the third day, he reads 15 pages more than the second day.

   6.____

If, on the following days, he continues to read at the same rate as he was reading on the third day, he will complete the report on the _____ day.
A. 7th  B. 8th  C. 10th  D. 11th

7. The 36 investigators in an agency are each required to submit 25 investigation reports a week. These reports are filled out on a certain form, and only one copy of the form is needed per report.
Allowing 20% for waste, how many packages of 45 forms a piece should be ordered for each weekly period?
A. 15  B. 20  C. 25  D. 30

8. During the fiscal year, an investigative unit received $260 for stationery and telephone expenditures. It spent 43% for stationery and 1/3 of the balance for telephone service.
The amount of money that was left at the end of the fiscal year was MOST NEARLY
A. $49  B. $50  C. $99  D. $109

Questions 9-10.

DIRECTIONS: Questions 9 and 10 are to be answered SOLELY on the data given below.

| Number of days absent per worker (sickness) | 1 | 2 | 3 | 4 | 5 | 6 | 7 | 8 or Over |
|---|---|---|---|---|---|---|---|---|
| Number of Workers | 96 | 45 | 16 | 3 | 1 | 0 | 1 | 0 |

Total Number of Workers: 500

9. The TOTAL number of man days lost due to illness in 2020 was
A. 137  B. 154  C. 162  D. 258

10. Of the 500 workers studied, the number who lost NO days due to sickness in 2020 was
A. 230  B. 298  C. 338  D. 372

Questions 11-13.

DIRECTIONS: Questions 11 through 13 are to be answered SOLELY on the basis of the following passage.

The rise of urban-industrial society has complicated the social arrangements needed to regulate contacts between people. As a consequence, there has been an unprecedented increase in the volume of laws and regulations designed to control individual conduct and to govern the relationship of the individual to others. In a century, there has been an eight-fold increase in the crimes for which one may be prosecuted.

For these offenses, the courts have the ultimate responsibility for redressing wrongs and convicting the guilty. The body of legal precepts gives the impression of an abstract and evenhanded dispensation of justice. Actually, the personnel of the agencies applying these precepts are faced with the difficulties of fitting abstract principles to highly variable situations emerging from the dynamics of everyday life. It is inevitable that discrepancies should exist between precept and practice.

The legal institutions serve as a framework for the social order by their slowness to respond to the caprices of transitory fad. This valuable contribution exacts a price in terms of the inflexibility of legal institutions in responding to new circumstances. This possibility is promoted by the changes in values and norms of the dynamic larger culture of which the legal precepts are a part.

11. According to the above passage, the increase in the number of laws and regulations during the twentieth century can be attributed to the
    A. complexity of modern industrial society
    B. increased seriousness of offenses committed
    C. growth of individualism
    D. anonymity of urban living

11.____

12. According to the above passage, which of the following presents a problem to the staff of legal agencies? The
    A. need to eliminate the discrepancy between precept and practice
    B. necessity to apply abstract legal precepts to rapidly changing conditions
    C. responsibility for reducing the number of abstract legal principles
    D. responsibility for understanding offenses in terms of the real-life situations from which they emerge

12.____

13. According to the above passage, it can be concluded that legal institutions affect social institutions by
    A. preventing change
    B. keeping pace with its norms and values
    C. changing its norms and values
    D. providing stability

13.____

Questions 14-16.

DIRECTIONS: Questions 14 through 16 are to be answered SOLELY on the basis of information given in the following passage.

A personnel interviewer, selecting job applicants, may find that he reacts badly to some people even on first contact. This reaction cannot usually be explained by things that the interviewee has done or said. Most of us have had the experience of liking or disliking, of feeling comfortable and uncomfortable with people on first acquaintance, long before we have had a chance to make a conscious, rational decision about them. Often, too, our liking or disliking is transmitted to the other person by subtle processes such as gestures, posture, voice intonations, or choice of words. The point to be kept in mind is this: the relations between people are complex and occur at several levels, from the conscious to the unconscious. This is true whether the relationship is brief or long, formal or informal.

Some of the major dynamics of personality which operate on the unconscious level are projection, sublimation, rationalization, and repression. Encountering these for the first time, one is apt to think of them as representing pathological states. In the extreme, they undoubtedly are, but they exist so universally that we must consider them also to be parts of normal personality.

Without necessarily subscribing to any of the numerous theories of personality, it is possible to describe personality in terms of certain important aspects or elements. We are all aware of ourselves as thinking organisms.

This aspect of personality, the conscious part, is important for understanding human behavior, but it is not enough. Many find it hard to accept the notion that each person also has an unconscious. The existence of the unconscious is no longer a matter of debate. It is not possible to estimate at all precisely what proportion of our total psychological life is conscious, what proportion unconscious. Everyone who has studied the problem, however, agrees that consciousness is the smaller part of personality. Most of what we are and do is a result of unconscious processes. To ignore this is to risk mistakes.

14. The above passage suggests that an interviewer can be MOST effective if he
    A. learns how to determine other peoples' unconscious motivations
    B. learns how to repress his own unconsciously motivated mannerisms and behavior
    C. can keep others from feeling that he either likes or dislikes them
    D. gains an understanding of how the unconscious operates in himself and in others

15. It may be inferred from the above passage that the *subtle processes*, such as gestures, posture, voice intonation, or choice of words referred to in the first paragraph are USUALLY
    A. in the complete control of an expert investigator
    B. the determining factors in the friendships a person establishes
    C. controlled by a person's unconscious
    D. not capable of being consciously controlled

16. The above passage implies that various different personality theories are USUALLY
    A. so numerous and different as to be valueless to an investigator
    B. in basic agreement about the importance of the unconscious
    C. understood by the investigator who strives to be effective
    D. in agreement that personality factors such as projection and repression are pathological

Questions 17-19.

DIRECTIONS: Questions 17 through 19 are to be answered SOLELY on the basis of information contained in the following passage.

No matter how well the interrogator adjusts himself to the witness and how precisely he induces the witness to describe his observations, mistakes still can be made. The mistakes made by an experienced interrogator may be comparatively few, but as far as the witness is concerned, his path is full of pitfalls. Modern "witness psychology" has shown that even the most honest and trustworthy witnesses are apt to make grave mistakes in good faith. It is, therefore, necessary that the interrogator get an idea of the weak links in the testimony in order to check up on them in the event that something appears to be strange or not quite satisfactory.

Unfortunately, modern witness psychology does not yet offer any means of directly testing the credibility of testimony. It lacks precision and method, in spite of worthwhile attempts on the part of learned men. At the same time, witness psychology, through the gathering of many experience concerning the weaknesses of human testimony, has been of invaluable service. It shows clearly that only evidence of a technical nature has absolute value as proof.

Testimony may be separated into the following stages: (1) perception; (2) observation; (3) mind fixation of the observed occurrences, in which fantasy, association of ideas, and personal judgment participate; (4) expression in oral or written form, where the testimony is transferred from one witness to another or to the interrogator. Each of these stages offers innumerable possibilities for the distortion of testimony.

17. The above passage indicates that having witnesses talk to each other before testifying is a practice which is GENERALLY
    A. *desirable*, since the witnesses will be able to correct each other's errors in observation before testimony
    B. *undesirable*, since the witnesses will collaborate on one story to tell the investigator
    C. *undesirable*, since one witness may distort his testimony because of what another witness may erroneously say
    D. *desirable*, since witnesses will become aware of discrepancies in their own testimony and can point out the discrepancies to the investigator

18. According to the above passage, the one of the following which would be the MOST reliable for use as evidence would be the testimony of a
    A. handwriting expert about a signature on a forged check
    B. trained police officer about the identity of a criminal
    C. laboratory technician about an accident he has observed
    D. psychologist who has interviewed any witness who relate conflicting stories

19. Concerning the validity of evidence, it is clear from the above passage that
    A. only evidence of a technical nature is at all valuable
    B. the testimony of witnesses is so flawed that it is usually valueless
    C. an investigator, by knowing modern witness psychology, will usually be able to perceive mistaken testimony
    D. an investigator ought to expect mistakes in even the most reliable witness testimony

Questions 20-21.

DIRECTIONS: Questions 20 and 21 are to be answered SOLELY on the basis of information given in the following passage.

Since we generally assure informants that what they say is confidential, we are not free to tell one informant what the other has told us. Even if the informant says, "*I don't care who knows it; tell anybody you want to,*" we find it wise to treat the interview as confidential. An interviewer who relates to some informants what other informants have told him is likely to stir up anxiety and suspicion. Of course, the interviewer may be able to tell an informant what he has heard without revealing the source of his information. This may be perfectly appropriate where a story has wide currency so that an informant cannot infer the source of the information. But if an event is not widely known, the mere mention of it may reveal to one informant what another informant has said about the situation. How can the data be cross-checked in these circumstances.

20. The above passage IMPLIES that the anxiety and suspicion an interviewer may arouse by telling what has been learned in other interviews is due to the    20.____
    A. lack of trust the person interviewed may have in the interviewer's honesty
    B. troublesome nature of the material which the interviewer has learned in other interviews
    C. fact that the person interviewed may not believe that permission was given to repeat the information
    D. fear of the person interviewed that what he is telling the interviewer will be repeated

21. The above passage is MOST likely part of a longer passage dealing with    21.____
    A. ways to verify data gathered in interviews
    B. the various anxieties a person being interviewed may feel
    C. the notion that people sometimes say things they do not mean
    D. ways an interview can avoid seeming suspicious

Questions 22-23.

DIRECTIONS: Questions 22 and 23 are to be answered SOLELY on the basis of information given below.

The ability to interview rests not on any single trait, but on a vast complex of them. Habits, skills, techniques, and attitudes are all involved. Competence in interviewing is acquired only after careful and diligent study, prolonged practice (preferably under supervision), and a good bit of trial and error; for interviewing is not an exact science; it is an art. Like many other arts, however, it can and must draw on science in several of its aspects.

There is always a place for individual initiative, for imaginative innovations, and for new combinations of old approaches. The skilled interviewer cannot be bound by a set of rules. Likewise, there is not a set of rules which can guarantee to the novice that his interviewing will be successful. There are, however, some accepted, general guideposts which may help the beginner to avoid mistakes, learn how to conserve this efforts, and establish effective working relationships with interviewees; to accomplish, in short, what he sets out to do.

22. According to the above passage, rules and standard techniques for interviewing are
    A. helpful for the beginner, but useless for the experienced, innovative interviewer
    B. destructive of the innovation and initiative needed for a good interviewer
    C. useful for even the experienced interviewer who may, however, sometimes go beyond them
    D. the means by which nearly anybody can become an effective interviewer

22.____

23. According to the above passage, the one of the following which is a prerequisite to competent interviewing is
    A. avoid mistakes
    B. study and practice
    C. imaginative innovation
    D. natural aptitude

23.____

Questions 24-27.

DIRECTIONS: Questions 24 through 27 are to be answered SOLELY on the basis of information given in the following passage.

The question of what material is relevant is not as simple as it might seem. Frequently, material which seems irrelevant to the inexperienced has, because of the common tendency to disguise and distort and misplace one's feelings, considerable significance. It may be necessary to let the client "ramble on" for a while in order to clear the decks, as it were, so that he may get down to things that really are on his mind. On the other hand, with an already disturbed person, it may be important for the interviewer to know when to discourage further elaboration of upsetting material. This is especially the case where the worker would be unable to do anything about it. An inexperienced interviewer might, for instance, be intrigued with the bizarre elaboration of material that the psychotic produces, but further elaboration of this might encourage the client in his instability. A too random discussion may indicate that the interviewee is not certain in what areas the interviewer is prepared to help him, and he may be seeking some direction. Or again, satisfying though it may be for the interviewer to have the interviewee tell him intimate details, such revelations sometimes need to be checked or encouraged only in small doses. An interviewee who has "talked too much" often reveals subsequent anxiety. This is illustrated by the fact that frequently after a "confessional" interview, the interviewee surprises the interviewer by being withdrawn, inarticulate, or hostile, or by breaking the next appointment.

24. Sometimes a client may reveal certain personal information to an interviewer and subsequently may feel anxious about this revelation.
    If, during an interview, a client begins to discuss very personal matters, it would be BEST to
    A. tell the client, in no uncertain terms, that you're not interested in personal details
    B. ignore the client at this point
    C. encourage the client to elaborate further on the details
    D. inform the client that the information seems to be very personal

24.____

25. The author indicates that clients with severe psychological disturbances pose an especially difficult problem for the inexperienced interviewer. The difficulty lies in the possibility of the client
    A. becoming physically violent and harming the interviewer
    B. rambling on for a while
    C. revealing irrelevant details which may be followed by cancelled appointments
    D. reverting to an unstable state as a result of interview material

26. An interviewer should be constantly alert to the possibility of obtaining clues from the client as to the problem areas.
    According to the above passage, a client who discusses topics at random may be
    A. unsure of what problems the interviewer can provide help with
    B. reluctant to discuss intimate details
    C. trying to impress the interviewer with his knowledge
    D. deciding what relevant material to elaborate on

27. The evaluation of a client's responses may reveal substantial information that may aid the interviewer in assessing the problem areas that are of concern to the client. Responses that seemed irrelevant at the time of the interview may be of significance because
    A. considerable significance is attached to all relevant material
    B. emotional feelings are frequently masked
    C. an initial *rambling on* is often a prelude to what is actually bothering the client
    D. disturbed clients often reveal subsequent anxiety

Questions 28-30.

DIRECTIONS: Questions 28 through 30 are to be answered SOLELY on the basis of the following passage.

The physical setting of the interview may determine its entire potentiality. Some degree of privacy and a comfortable relaxed atmosphere are important. The interviewee is not encouraged to give much more than his name and address if the interviewer seems busy with other things, if people are rushing about, if there are distracting noises. He has a right to feel that, whether the interview lasts five minutes or an hour, he has, for that time, the undivided attention of the interviewer. Interruptions, telephone calls, and so on, should be reduced to a minimum. If the interviewee has waited in a crowded room for what seems to him an interminably long period, he is naturally in mood to sit down and discuss what is on his mind. Indeed, by that time, the primary thing on his mind may be his irritation at being kept waiting, and he frequently feels it would be impolite to express this. If a wait or interruptions have been unavoidable, it is always helpful to give the client some recognition that these are disturbing and that we can naturally understand that they make it more difficult for him to proceed. At the same time, if he protests that they have not troubled him, the interviewer can best accept his statements at their face value, as further insistence that they must have been disturbing may be interpreted by him as accusing, and he may conclude that the interviewer has been personally hurt by his irritation.

28. Distraction during an interview may tend to limit the client's responses. In a case where an interruption has occurred, it would be BEST for the investigator to
    A. terminate this interview and have it rescheduled for another time period
    B. ignore the interruption since it is not continuous
    C. express his understanding that the distraction can cause the client to feel disturbed
    D. accept the client's protests that he has been troubled by the interruption

29. To maximize the rapport that can be established with the client, an appropriate physical setting is necessary. At the very least, some privacy would be necessary.
    In addition, the interviewer should
    A. always appear to be busy in order to impress the client
    B. focus his attention only on the client
    C. accept all the client's statements as being valid
    D. stress the importance of the interview to the client

30. Clients who have been waiting quite some time for their interview may, justifiably, become upset.
    However, a client may initially attempt to mask these feelings because he may
    A. personally hurt the interviewer
    B. want to be civil
    C. feel that the wait was unavoidable
    D. fear the consequences of his statement

## KEY (CORRECT ANSWERS)

| | | | | | |
|---|---|---|---|---|---|
| 1. | B | 11. | A | 21. | A |
| 2. | C | 12. | B | 22. | C |
| 3. | D | 13. | D | 23. | B |
| 4. | D | 14. | D | 24. | D |
| 5. | B | 15. | C | 25. | D |
| 6. | D | 16. | B | 26. | A |
| 7. | C | 17. | C | 27. | B |
| 8. | C | 18. | A | 28. | C |
| 9. | D | 19. | D | 29. | B |
| 10. | C | 20. | D | 30. | B |

# TEST 2

DIRECTIONS: Each question or incomplete statement is followed by several suggested answers or completions. Select the one that BEST answers the question or completes the statement. *PRINT THE LETTER OF THE CORRECT ANSWER IN THE SPACE AT THE RIGHT.*

Questions 1-5.

DIRECTIONS: In Questions 1 through 5, choose the statement which is BEST from the point of view of English usage suitable for a business report.

1. 
   A. The client's receiving of public assistance checks at two different addresses were disclosed by the investigation.
   B. The investigation disclosed that the client was receiving public assistance checks at two different addresses.
   C. The client was found out by the investigator to be receiving public assistance checks at two different addresses.
   D. The client has been receiving public assistance checks at two different addresses, disclosed the investigation

   1.____

2. 
   A. The investigation of complaints are usually handled by this unit, which deals with internal security problems in the department.
   B. This unit deals with internal security problems in the department; usually investigating complaints.
   C. Investigating complaints is this unit's job, being that it handles internal security problems in the department
   D. This unit deals with internal security problems in the department and usually investigates complaints.

   2.____

3. 
   A. The delay in completing this investigation was caused by difficulty in obtaining the required documents from the candidate.
   B. Because of difficulty in obtaining the required documents from the candidate is the reason that there was a delay in completing this investigation.
   C. Having had difficulty in obtaining the required documents from the candidate, there was a delay in completing this investigation.
   D. Difficulty in obtaining the required documents from the candidate had the affect of delaying the completion of this investigation.

   3.____

4. 
   A. This report, together with documents supporting our recommendation, are being submitted for your approval.
   B. Documents supporting our recommendation is being submitted with the report for your approval.
   C. This report, together with documents supporting our documentation, is being submitted for your approval.
   D. The report and documents supporting our recommendation is being submitted for your approval.

   4.____

5.  A. Several people were interviewed and numerous letters were sent before this case was completed.   5._____
    B. Completing this case, interviewing several people and sending numerous letters were necessary.
    C. To complete this case needed interviewing several people and sending numerous letters.
    D. Interviewing several people and sending numerous letters was necessary to complete the case.

Questions 6-20.

DIRECTIONS: For each of the sentences numbered 6 to 20, select from the options given below the MOST applicable choice, and mark your answer accordingly.
   A. The sentence is correct.
   B. The sentence contains a spelling error only.
   C. The sentence contains an English grammar error only.
   D. The sentence contains both a spelling error and an English grammar error.

6. He is a very dependable person whom we expect will be an asset to this division.   6._____

7. An investigator often finds it necessary to be very diplomatic when conducting an interview.   7._____

8. Accurate detail is especially important if court action results from an investigation.   8._____

9. The report was signed by him and I since we conducted the investigation jointly.   9._____

10. Upon receipt of the complaint, an inquiry was begun.   10._____

11. An employee has to organize his time so that he can handle his workload efficiantly.   11._____

12. It was not apparent that anyone was living at the address given by the client.   12._____

13. According to regulations, there is to be at least three attempts made to locate the client.   13._____

14. Neither the inmate nor the correction officer was willing to sign a formal statement.   14._____

15. It is our opinion that one of the persons interviewed were lying.   15._____

16. We interviewed both clients and departmental personel in the course of this investigation.   16._____

17. It is concievable that further research might produce additional evidence.   17._____

18. There are too many occurences of this nature to ignore.   18._____

19. We cannot accede to the candidate's request.                                          19._____

20. The submission of overdue reports is the reason that there was a delay in              20._____
    completion of this investigation.

Questions 21-2.

DIRECTIONS:  Each of Questions 21 through 25 consists of three sentences lettered A, B, and
             C.  In each of these questions, one of the sentences may contain an error in
             grammar, sentence structure, or punctuation, or all three sentences may be
             correct.  If one of the sentences in a question contains an error in grammar,
             sentence structure, or punctuation, print in the space at the right the capital
             letter preceding the sentence which contains the error.  If all three sentences
             are correct, print the letter D.

21. A.  Mr. Smith appears to be less competent than I in performing these duties.          21._____
    B.  The supervisor spoke to the employee, who had made the error, but did
        not reprimand him.
    C.  When he found the book lying on the table, he immediately notified the
        owner.

22. A.  Being locked in the desk, we were certain that the papers would not be             22._____
        taken.
    B.  It wasn't I who dictated the telegram; I believe it was Eleanor.
    C.  You should interview whoever comes to the office today.

23. A.  The clerk was instructed to set the machine on the table before                    23._____
        summoning the manager.
    B.  He said that he was not familiar with those kind of activities.
    C.  A box of pencils, in addition to erasers and blotters, was included in the
        shipment.

24. A.  The supervisor remarked, "Assigning an employee to the proper type of              24._____
        work is not always easy."
    B.  The employer found that each of the applicants were qualified to perform
        the duties of the position.
    C.  Any competent student is permitted to take this course if he obtains the
        consent of the instructor.

25. A.  The prize was awarded to the employee whom the judges believed to be               25._____
        most deserving.
    B.  Since the instructor believes this book is the better of the two, he is
        recommending it for use in the school.
    C.  It was obvious to the employees that the completion of the task by the
        scheduled date would require their working overtime.

## KEY (CORRECT ANSWERS)

1. B
2. D
3. A
4. C
5. A

6. D
7. A
8. A
9. C
10. A

11. B
12. B
13. C
14. A
15. C

16. B
17. B
18. B
19. A
20. C

21. B
22. A
23. B
24. B
25. D

# EXAMINATION SECTION
## TEST 1

DIRECTIONS: Each question or incomplete statement is followed by several suggested answers or completions. Select the one that BEST answers the question or completes the statement. *PRINT THE LETTER OF THE CORRECT ANSWER IN THE SPACE AT THE RIGHT.*

1. Following are three statements concerning on-the-job training:
   I. On-the-job training is rarely used as a method of training employees.
   II. On-the-job training is often carried on with little or no planning.
   III. On-the-job training is often less expensive than other types.
   Which of the following BEST classifies the above statements into those that are correct and those that are not?
   A. I is correct, but II and III are not.  B. II is correct but I and III are not.
   C. I and II are correct, but III is not.  D. II and III are correct, but I is not.

   1.____

2. The one of the following which is NOT a valid principle for a supervisor to keep in mind when talking to a subordinate about his performance is:
   A. People frequently know when they deserve criticism.
   B. Supervisors should be prepared to offer suggestions to subordinates about how to improve their work.
   C. Good points should be discussed before bad points.
   D. Magnifying a subordinate's faults will get him to improve faster.

   2.____

3. In many organizations information travels quickly through the grapevine. Following are three statements concerning the *grapevine*:
   I. Information a subordinate does not want to tell her supervisor may reach the supervisor through the *grapevine*.
   II. A supervisor can often do her job better by knowing the information that travels through the *grapevine*.
   III. A supervisor can depend on the *grapevine* as a way to get accurate information from the employees on his staff.
   Which one of the following CORRECTLY classifies the above statements into those which are generally correct and those which are not?
   A. II is correct, but I and III are not.  B. III is correct, but I and II are not.
   C. I and II are correct, but III is not.  D. I and III are correct, but II is not.

   3.____

4. Following are three statements concerning supervision:
   I. A supervisor knows he is doing a good job if his subordinates depend upon him to make every decision.
   II. A supervisor who delegates authority to his subordinates soon finds that his subordinates begin to resent him.
   III. Giving credit for good work is frequently an effective method of getting subordinates to work harder

   4.____

Which one of the following CORRECTLY classifies the above statements into those that are correct and those that are not?
- A. I and II are correct, but III is not.
- B. II and III are correct, but I is not.
- C. II is correct, but I and III are not.
- D. III is correct, but I and II are not.

5. Of the following, the LEAST appropriate action for a supervisor to take in preparing a disciplinary case against a subordinate is to
   - A. keep careful records of each incident in which the subordinate has been guilty of misconduct or incompetency, even though immediate disciplinary action may not be necessary
   - B. discuss with the employee each incident of misconduct as it occurs so the employee knows where he stands
   - C. accept memoranda from any other employees who may have been witnesses to acts of misconduct
   - D. keep the subordinate's personnel file confidential so that he is unaware of the evidence being gathered against him

6. Praise by a supervisor can be an important element in motivating subordinates. Following are three statements concerning a supervisor's praise of subordinates:
   I. In order to be effective, praise must be lavish and constantly restated.
   II. Praise should be given in a manner which meets the needs of the individual subordinate.
   III. The subordinate whose work is praised should believe that the praise is earned.

   Which of the following CORRECTLY classifies the above statements into those that are correct and those that are not?
   - A. I is correct, but II and III are not.
   - B. II and III are correct, but I is not.
   - C. III is correct, but I and II are not.
   - D. I and II are correct, but III is not.

7. A supervisor feels that he is about to lose his temper while reprimanding a subordinate.
   Of the following, the BEST action for the supervisor to take is to
   - A. postpone the reprimand for a short time until his self-control is assured
   - B. continue the reprimand because a loss of temper by the supervisor will show the subordinate the seriousness of the error he made
   - C. continue the reprimand because failure to do so will show that the supervisor does not have complete self-control
   - D. postpone the reprimand until the subordinate is capable of understanding the reason for the supervisor's loss of temper

8. Following are three statements concerning various ways of giving orders to subordinates:
   I. An implied order or suggestion is usually appropriate for the inexperienced employee.
   II. A polite request is less likely to upset a sensitive subordinate than a direct order.
   III. A direct order is usually appropriate in an emergency situation.

Which of the following CORRECTLY classifies the above statements into those that are correct and those that are not?
- A. I is correct, but II and III are not.
- B. II and III are correct, but I is not.
- C. III is correct, but I and II are not.
- D. I and II are correct, but III is not.

9. The one of the following which is NOT an acceptable reason for taking disciplinary action against a subordinate guilty of serious violations of the rules is that
   - A. the supervisor can *let off steam* against subordinates who break rules frequently
   - B. a subordinate whose work continues to be unsatisfactory may be terminated
   - C. a subordinate may be encouraged to improve his work
   - D. an example is set for other employees

10. At the first meeting with your staff after appointment as a supervisor, you find considerable indifference and some hostility among the participants.
    Of the following, the MOST appropriate way to handle this situation is to
    - A. disregard the attitudes displayed and continue to make your presentation until you have completed it
    - B. discontinue your presentation but continue the meeting and attempt to find out the reasons for their attitudes
    - C. warm up your audience with some good-natured statements and anecdotes and then proceed with your presentation
    - D. discontinue the meeting and set up personal interviews with the staff members to try to find out the reason for their attitude

11. Use a written rather than oral communication to amend any previous written communication.
    Of the following, the BEST justification for this statement is that
    - A. oral changes will be considered more impersonal and thus less important
    - B. oral changes will be forgotten or recalled indifferently
    - C. written communications are clearer and shorter
    - D. written communications are better able to convey feeling tone

12. Assume that a certain supervisor, when writing important communications to his subordinates, often repeats certain points in different words.
    This technique is GENERALLY
    - A. *ineffective*; it tends to confuse rather than help
    - B. *effective*; it tends to improve understanding by the subordinates
    - C. *ineffective*; it unnecessarily increases the length of the communication and may annoy the subordinates
    - D. *effective*; repetition is always an advantage in communications

13. In preparing a letter or a report, a supervisor may wish to persuade the reader of the correctness of some idea or course of action.
    The BEST way to accomplish this is for the supervisor to
    - A. encourage the reader to make a prompt decision
    - B. express each idea in a separate paragraph

C. present the subject matter of the letter in the first paragraph
D. state the potential benefits for the reader

14. Effective communications, a basic necessity for successful supervision is a two-way street. A good supervisor needs to listen to, as well as disseminate, information and he must be able to encourage his subordinates to communicate with him.
Which of the following suggestions will contribute LEAST to improving the *listening power* of a supervisor?
   A. Don't assume anything; don't anticipate, and don't let a subordinate think you know what he is going to say
   B. Don't interrupt; let him have his full say even if it requires a second session that day to get the full story
   C. React quickly to his statements so that he knows you are interested, even if you must draw some conclusions prematurely
   D. Try to understand the real need for his talking to you even if it is quite different from the subject under discussion

15. Of the following, the MOST useful approach for the supervisor to take toward the informal employee communications network known as the *grapevine* is to
   A. remain isolated from it, but not take any active steps to eliminate it
   B. listen to it, but not depend on it for accurate information
   C. use it to disseminate confidential information
   D. eliminate it as diplomatically as possible

16. If a supervisor is asked to estimate the number of employees that he believes he will need in his unit in the coming fiscal year, the supervisor should FIRST attempt to learn the
   A. nature and size of the workload his unit will have during that time
   B. cost of hiring and training new employees
   C. average number of employee absences per year
   D. number of employees needed to indirectly support or assist his unit

17. An important supervisory responsibility is coordinating the operations of the unit. This may include setting work schedules, controlling work quality, establishing interim due dates, etc. In order to handle this task, it has been divided into the following five stages:
   I. Determine the steps or sequence required for the tasks to be performed.
   II. Give the orders, either written or oral, to begin work on the tasks.
   III. Check up by following each task to make sure it is proceeding according to plan.
   IV. Schedule the jobs by setting a time for each task of operation to begin and end.
   V. Control the process by correcting conditions which interfere with the plan.
The MOST logical sequence in which these planning steps should be performed is:
   A. I, II, III, IV, V   B. II, I, V, III, IV   C. I, IV, II, III, V   D. IV, I, II, III, V

18. Assume that a supervisor calls a meeting with the staff under his supervision in order to discuss several proposals. After some discussion, he realizes that he strongly disagrees with one proposal that four of the staff have rather firmly favored.
At this point, he could BEST handle the situation by saying:
   A. *I have the responsibility for this decision, and I must disagree.*
   B. *I am just reminding you that I have had a great deal more experience in these matters.*
   C. *You have presented some good points, but perhaps we could look at it another way.*
   D. *The only way that this proposal can be disposed of is to defer it for further discussion.*

18.____

19. As far as the social activities and groups of his subordinates are concerned, a supervisor in a large organization can BEST strengthen his tools of leadership by
   A. emphasizing the organization as a whole and forbidding the formation of groups
   B. ignoring the groups as much as possible and dealing with each subordinate as an individual
   C. learning about the status structure of employee groups and their values
   D. avoiding any relationship with groups

19.____

20. If a subordinate asks you, his superior, for advice in planning his career in the department, you should
   A. encourage him to feel that he can easily reach the top of his occupational ladder
   B. discourage him from setting his hopes too high
   C. discuss career opportunities realistically with him
   D. explain that you have no control over his opportunities for advancement

20.____

21. A supervisor's evaluation of an employee is usually based upon a combination of objective facts and subjective judgments or opinions.
Which of the following aspects of an employee's work or performance is MOST likely to be subjectively evaluated?
   A. Quantity      B. Accuracy      C. Attitude      D. Attendance

21.____

22. Of the following possible characteristics of supervisors, the one MOST likely to lead to failure as a supervisor is
   A. a tendency to seek several opinions before making decisions in complex matters
   B. lack of a strong desire to advance to a top position in management
   C. little formal training in human relations skills
   D. poor relations with subordinates and other supervisory personnel

22.____

23. People who break rules do so for a number of reasons. However, employees will break rules LESS often if
    A. the supervisor uses his own judgment about work methods
    B. the supervisor pretends to act strictly, but isn't really serious about it
    C. they greatly enjoy their work
    D. they have completed many years of service

24. Assume that an employee under your supervision has become resentful and generally non-cooperative after his request for transfer to another office closer to his place of residence was denied. The request was denied primarily because of the importance of his current assignment. The employee has been a valued worker, but you are now worried that his resentful attitude will have a detrimental effect.
    Of the following, the MOST desirable way for you to handle this situation is to
    A. arrange for the employee's transfer to the office he originally requested
    B. arrange for the employee's transfer to another office, but not the one he originally requested
    C. attempt to re-focus the employee's attention on those aspects of his current assignment which will be most rewarding and satisfying to him
    D. explain to the employee that, while you are sympathetic to his request, department rules will not allow transfers for reasons of personal convenience

25. Of the following, it would be LEAST advisable for a supervisor to use his administrative authority to affect the behavior and activities of his subordinates when he is trying to
    A. change the way his subordinates perform a particular task
    B. establish a minimum level of conformity to established rules
    C. bring about change in the attitudes of his subordinates
    D. improve the speed with which his subordinates respond to his orders

26. Assume that a supervisor gives his subordinate instructions which are appropriate and clear. The subordinate thereupon refuses to follow these instructions.
    Of the following, it would then be MOST appropriate for the supervisor to
    A. attempt to find out what it is that the employee objects to
    B. take disciplinary action that same day
    C. remind the subordinate about supervisory authority and threaten him with discipline
    D. insist that the subordinate carry out the order immediately

27. Of the following, the MOST effective way to identify training needs resulting from gradual changes in procedure is to
    A. monitor on a continuous basis the actual jobs performed and the skills required
    B. periodically send out a written questionnaire asking personnel to identify their needs
    C. conduct interviews at regular intervals with selected employees
    D. consult employees' personnel records

28. Assume that you, as a supervisor, have had a new employee assigned to you. If the duties of his position can be broken into independent parts, which of the following is usually the BEST way to train this new employee?
Start with
    A. the easiest duties and progressively proceed to the most difficult
    B. something easy; move to something difficult; then back to something easy
    C. something difficult; move to something easy; then to something difficult
    D. the most difficult duties and progressively proceed to the easiest

29. The oldest and most commonly used training technique is on-the-job training. Instruction is given to the worker by his supervisor or by another employee. Such training is essential in most jobs, although it is not always effective when used alone.
This technique, however, can be effectively used alone if
    A. the skills involved can be learned quickly
    B. a large number of people are to be trained at one time
    C. other forms of training have not been previously used with the people involved
    D. the skills to be taught are mental rather than manual

30. It is generally agreed that the learning process is facilitated in proportion to the amount of feedback that the learner is given about his performance.
Following are three statements concerning the learning process:
    I. The more specific the learner's knowledge of how he performed, the more rapid his improvement and the higher his level of performance
    II. Giving the learner knowledge of his results does not affect his motivation to learn.
    III. Learners who are not given feedback will set up subjective criteria and evaluate their own performance.
Which of the following choices lists ALL of the above statements that are generally CORRECT?
    A. I and II only     B. I and III only     C. II and III only     D. I, II, and III

## KEY (CORRECT ANSWERS)

| | | | | | |
|---|---|---|---|---|---|
| 1. | D | 11. | B | 21. | C |
| 2. | D | 12. | B | 22. | D |
| 3. | C | 13. | D | 23. | C |
| 4. | D | 14. | C | 24. | C |
| 5. | D | 15. | B | 25. | C |
| | | | | | |
| 6. | B | 16. | A | 26. | A |
| 7. | A | 17. | C | 27. | A |
| 8. | B | 18. | C | 28. | A |
| 9. | A | 19. | C | 29. | A |
| 10. | D | 20. | C | 30. | B |

# TEST 2

DIRECTIONS: Each question or incomplete statement is followed by several suggested answers or completions. Select the one that BEST answers the question or completes the statement. *PRINT THE LETTER OF THE CORRECT ANSWER IN THE SPACE AT THE RIGHT.*

Questions 1-6.

DIRECTIONS: Questions 1 through 6 are to be answered SOLELY on the basis of the information given in the following paragraph.

The use of role-playing as a training technique was developed during the past decade by social scientists, particularly psychologists, who have been active in training experiments. Originally, this technique was applied by clinical psychologists who discovered that a patient appears to gain understanding of an emotionally disturbing situation when encouraged to act out roles in that situation. As applied in government and business organizations, the purpose of role-playing is to aid employees to understand certain work problems involving interpersonal relations and to enable observers to evaluate various reactions to them. Thus, for example, on the problem of handling grievances, two individuals from the group might be selected to act out extemporaneously the parts of subordinate and supervisor. When this situation is enacted by various pairs among the class and the techniques and results are discussed, the members of the group are presumed to reach conclusions about the most effective means of handling similar situations. Often the use of role reversal, where participants take parts different from their actual work roles, assists individuals to gain more insight into other people's problems and viewpoints. Although role-playing can be a rewarding training device, the trainer must be aware of his responsibilities. If this technique is to be successful, thorough briefing of both actors and observers as to the situation in question, the participants' roles, and what to look for, is essential.

1. The role-playing technique was FIRST used for the purpose of
    A. measuring the effectiveness of training programs
    B. training supervisors in business organizations
    C. treating emotionally disturbed patients
    D. handling employee grievances

1.____

2. When role-playing is used in private business as a training device, the CHIEF aim is to
    A. develop better relations between supervisor and subordinate in the handling of grievances
    B. come up with a solution to a specific problem that has arisen
    C. determine the training needs of the group
    D. increase employee understanding of the human relation factors in work situations

2.____

3. From the above passage, it is MOST reasonable to conclude that when role-playing is used, it is preferable to have the roles acted out by
    A. only one set of actors
    B. no more than 2 sets of actors
    C. several different sets of actors
    D. the trainer or trainers of the group

3.____

4. Based on the above passage, a trainer using the technique of role reversal in a problem of first-line supervision should assign a senior employee to play the part of a(n)
    A. new employee
    B. senior employee
    C. principal employee
    D. angry citizen

4.____

5. It can be inferred from the above passage that a limitation of role-play as a training method is that
    A. many work situations do not lend themselves to role-play
    B. employees are not experienced enough as actors to play the roles realistically
    C. only trainers who have psychological training can use it successfully
    D. participants who are observing and not acting do not benefit from it

5.____

6. To obtain good results from the use of role-playing in training, a trainer should give participants
    A. a minimum of information about the situation so that they can act spontaneously
    B. scripts which illustrate the best method for handling the situation
    C. a complete explanation of the problem and the roles to be acted out
    D. a summary of work problems which involve interpersonal relations

6.____

7. Of the following, the MOST important reason for a supervisor to prepare good written reports is that
    A. a supervisor is rated on the quality of his reports
    B. decisions are often made on the basis of the reports
    C. such reports take less time for superiors to review
    D. such reports demonstrate efficiency of department operations

7.____

8. Of the following, the BEST test of a good report is whether it
    A. provides the information needed
    B. shows the good sense of the writer
    C. is prepared according to a proper format
    D. is grammatical and neat

8.____

9. When a supervisor writes a report, he can BEST show that he has an understanding of the subject of the report by
    A. including necessary facts and omitting non-essential details
    B. using statistical data
    C. giving his conclusions but not the data on which they are based
    D. using a technical vocabulary

9.____

10. Suppose you and another supervisor on the same level are assigned to work together on a report. You disagree strongly with one of the recommendations the other supervisor wants to include in the report but you cannot change his views.
    Of the following, it would be BEST that
    A. you refuse to accept responsibility for the report
    B. you ask that someone else be assigned to this project to replace you

10.____

C. each of you state his own ideas about this recommendation in the report
D. you give in to the other supervisor's opinion for the sake of harmony

11. Standardized forms are often provided for submitting reports.
    Of the following, the MOST important advantage of using standardized forms for reports is that
    A. they take less time to prepare than individually written reports
    B. necessary information is less likely to be omitted
    C. the responsibility for preparing these reports can be delegated to subordinates
    D. the person making the report can omit information he considers unimportant

12. A report which may BEST be classed as a *periodic* report is one which
    A. requires the same type of information at regular intervals
    B. contains detailed information which is to be retained in permanent records
    C. is prepared whenever a special situation occurs
    D. lists information in graphic form

13. Which one of the following is NOT an important reason for keeping accurate records in an office?
    A. Facts will be on hand when decisions have to be made.
    B. The basis for past actions can be determined.
    C. Information needed by other bureaus can be furnished.
    D. Filing is easier when records are properly made out.

14. Suppose you are preparing to write a report recommending a change in a certain procedure. You learn that another supervisor made a report a few years ago suggesting a change in this same procedure, but that no action was taken.
    Of the following, it would be MOST desirable for you to
    A. avoid reading the other supervisor's report so that you will write with a more up-to-date point of view
    B. make no recommendation since management seems to be against any change in the procedure
    C. read the other report before you write your report to see what bearing it may have on your recommendations
    D. avoid including in your report any information that can be obtained by referring to the other report

15. If a report you are preparing to your superior is going to be a very long one, it would be DESIRABLE to include a summary of your basic conclusions
    A. at the end of the report
    B. at the beginning of the report
    C. in a separate memorandum
    D. right after you present the supporting data

16. Suppose that some bureau and department policies must be very frequently applied by your subordinates while others rarely come into use.
    As a supervising employee, a GOOD technique for you to use in fulfilling your responsibility of seeing to it that policies are adhered to is to
    A. ask the director of the bureau to issue to all employees an explanation in writing of all policies
    B. review with your subordinates every week those policies which have daily application
    C. follow up on and explain at regular intervals the application of those policies which are not used very often by your subordinates
    D. recommend to your superiors that policies rarely used be changed or dropped

17. The BASIC purpose behind the principle of delegation of authority is to
    A. give the supervisor who is delegating a chance to acquire skills in higher level functions
    B. free the supervisor from routine tasks in order that he may do the important parts of his job
    C. prevent supervisors from overstepping the lines of authority which have been established
    D. place the work delegated in the hands of those employees who can perform it best

18. A district commander can BEST assist management in long-range planning by
    A. reporting to his superiors any changing conditions in the district
    B. maintaining a neat and efficiently run office
    C. scheduling work so that areas with a high rate of non-compliance get more intensive coverage
    D. properly training new personnel assigned to his district

19. Suppose that new quarters have been rented for your district office.
    Of the following, the LEAST important factor to be considered in planning the layout of the office is the
    A. need for screening confidential activities from unauthorized persons
    B. relative importance of the various types of work
    C. areas of noise concentration
    D. convenience with which communication between sections of the office can be achieved

20. Of the following, the MOST basic effect of organizing a department so that lines of authority are clearly defined and duties are specifically assigned is to
    A. increase the need for close supervision
    B. decreases the initiative of subordinates
    C. lessen the possibility of duplication of work
    D. increase the responsibilities of supervisory personnel

21. An accepted management principle is that decisions should be delegated to the lowest point in the organization at which they can be made effectively.
    The one of the following which is MOST likely to be a result of the application of this principle is that
    A. no factors will be overlooked in making decisions
    B. prompt action will follow the making of decisions
    C. decisions will be made more rapidly
    D. coordination of decisions that are made will be simplified

21.____

22. Suppose you are a supervisor and need some guidance from a higher authority. In which one of the following situations would it be PERMISSIBLE for you to bypass the regular upward channels of communication in the chain of command?
    A. In an emergency when your superior is not available
    B. When it is not essential to get a quick reply
    C. When you feel your immediate superior is not understanding of the situation
    D. When you want to obtain information that you think your superior does not have

22.____

23. Of the following, the CHIEF limitation of the organization chart as it is generally used in business and government is that the chart
    A. makes lines of responsibility and authority undesirably definite and formal
    B. is often out of date as soon as it is completed
    C. does not show human factors and informal working relationships
    D. is usually too complicated

23.____

24. The *span of control* for any supervisor is the
    A. number of tasks he is expected to perform himself
    B. amount of office space he and his subordinates occupy
    C. amount of work he is responsible for getting out
    D. number of subordinates he can supervise effectively

24.____

25. Of the following duties performed by a supervising employee, which would be considered a LINE function rather than a staff function?
    A. Evaluation of office personnel
    B. Recommendations for disciplinary action
    C. Initiating budget requests for replacement of equipment
    D. Inspections, at irregular times, of conditions and staff in the field

25.____

## KEY (CORRECT ANSWERS)

| | | | |
|---|---|---|---|
| 1. | C | 11. | B |
| 2. | D | 12. | A |
| 3. | C | 13. | D |
| 4. | A | 14. | C |
| 5. | A | 15. | B |
| 6. | C | 16. | C |
| 7. | B | 17. | B |
| 8. | A | 18. | A |
| 9. | A | 19. | B |
| 10. | C | 20. | C |

21. B
22. A
23. C
24. D
25. D

# EXAMINATION SECTION
# TEST 1

DIRECTIONS: Each question or incomplete statement is followed by several suggested answers or completions. Select the one that BEST answers the question or completes the statement. *PRINT THE LETTER OF THE CORRECT ANSWER IN THE SPACE AT THE RIGHT.*

1. An interview is BEST conducted in private primarily because
    A. the person interviewed will tend to be less self-conscious
    B. the interviewer will be able to maintain his continuity of thought better
    C. it will insure that the interview is "off the record"
    D. people tend to "show off" before an audience

2. An interviewer can BEST establish a good relationship with the person being interviewed by
    A. assuming casual interest in the statements made by the person being interviewed
    B. taking the point of view of the person interviewed
    C. controlling the interview to a major extent
    D. showing a genuine interest in the person

3. An interviewer will be better able to understand the person interviewed and his problems if he recognizes that much of the person's behavior is due to motives
    A. which are deliberate
    B. of which he is unaware
    C. which are inexplicable
    D. which are kept under control

4. An interviewer's attention must be directed toward himself as well as toward the person interviewed.
    This statement means that the interviewer should
    A. keep in mind the extent to which his own prejudices may influence his judgment
    B. rationalize the statements made by the person interviewed
    C. gain the respect and confidence of the person interviewed
    D. avoid being too impersonal

5. More complete expression will be obtained from a person being interviewed if the interviewer can create the impression that
    A. the data secured will become part of a permanent record
    B. official information must be accurate in every detail
    C. it is the duty of the person interviewed to give accurate data
    D. the person interviewed is participating in a discussion of his own problems

6. The practice of asking leading questions should be avoided in an interview because the
   A. interviewer risks revealing his attitudes to the person being interviewed
   B. interviewer may be led to ignore the objective attitudes of the person interviewed
   C. answers may be unwarrantedly influenced
   D. person interviewed will resent the attempt to lead him and will be less cooperative

7. A good technique for the interviewer to use in an effort to secure reliable data and to reduce the possibility of misunderstanding is to
   A. use casual undirected conversation, enabling the person being interviewed to talk about himself, and thus secure the desired information
   B. adopt the procedure of using direct questions regularly
   C. extract the desired information from the person being interviewed by putting him on the defensive
   D. explain to the person being interviewed the information desired and the reason for needing it

8. You are interviewing a patient to determine whether she is eligible for medical assistance. Of the many questions that you have to ask her, some are routine questions that patients tend to answer willingly and easily. Other questions are more personal and some patients tend to resent being asked them and avoid answering them directly.
   For you to begin the interview with the more personal questions would be
   A. *desirable*, because the end of the interview will go smoothly and the patient will be left with a warm feeling
   B. *undesirable*, because the patient might not know the answers to the questions
   C. *desirable*, because you will be able to return to these questions later to verify the accuracy of the responses
   D. *undesirable*, because you might antagonize the patient before you have had a chance to establish rapport

9. While interviewing a patient about her family composition, the patient asks you whether you are married.
   Of the following, the MOST appropriate way for you to handle this situation is to
   A. answer the question briefly and redirect her back to the topic under discussion
   B. refrain from answering the question and proceed with the interview
   C. advise the patient that it is more important that she answer your questions than that you answer hers, and proceed with the interview
   D. promise the patient that you will answer her question later, in the hope that she will forget, and redirect her back to the topic under discussion

10. In response to a question about his employment history, a patient you are interviewing rambles and talks about unrelated matters.
    Of the following, the MOST appropriate course of action for you to take FIRST is to

A. ask questions to direct the patient back to his employment history
B. advise him to concentrate on your questions and not to discuss irrelevant information
C. ask him why he is resisting a discussion of his employment history
D. advise him that if you cannot get the information you need, he will not be eligible for medical assistance

11. Suppose that a person you are interviewing becomes angry at some of the questions you have asked, calls you meddlesome and nosy, and states that she will not answer those questions.
Of the following, which is the BEST action for you to take?
A. Explain the reasons the questions are asked and the importance of the answers
B. Inform the interviewee that you are only doing your job and advise her that she should answer your questions or leave the office
C. Report to your supervisor what the interviewee called you and refuse to continue the interview
D. End the interview and tell the interviewee she will not be serviced by your department

11.____

12. Suppose that during the course of an interview the interviewee demands in a very rude way that she be permitted to talk to your supervisor or someone in charge.
Which of the following is probably the BEST way to handle this situation?
A. Inform your supervisor of the demand and ask her to speak to the interviewee
B. Pay no attention to the demands of the interviewee and continue the interview
C. Report to your supervisor and tell her to get another interviewer for this interviewee
D. Tell her you are the one "in charge" and that she should talk to you

12.____

13. Of the following, the outcome of an interview by an aide depends MOST heavily on the
A. personality of the interviewee
B. personality of the aide
C. subject matter of the questions asked
D. interaction between aide and interviewee

13.____

14. Some patients being interviewed are primarily interested in making a favorable impression.
The aide should be aware of the fact that such patients are more likely than other patients to
A. try to anticipate the answers the interviewer is looking for
B. answer all questions openly and frankly
C. try to assume the role of interviewer
D. be anxious to get the interview over as quickly as possible

14.____

15. The type of interview which an aide usually conducts is substantially different from most interviewing situations in all of the following aspects EXCEPT the
    A. setting
    B. kinds of clients
    C. techniques employed
    D. kinds of problems

15.____

16. During an interview, an aide uses a "leading question."
    This type of question is so-called because it generally
    A. starts a series of questions about one topic
    B. suggests the answer which the aide wants
    C. forms the basis for a following "trick" question
    D. sets, at the beginning, the tone of the interview

16.____

17. Casework interviewing is always directed to the client and his situation.
    The one of the following which is the MOST accurate statement with respect to the proper focus of an interview is that the
    A. caseworker limits the client to concentration on objective data
    B. client is generally permitted to talk about facts and feelings with no direction from the caseworker
    C. main focus in casework interviews is on feelings rather than facts
    D. caseworker is responsible for helping the client focus on any material which seems to be related to his problems or difficulties

17.____

18. Assume that you are conducting a training program for the caseworkers under your supervision. At one of the sessions, you discuss the problem of interviewing a dull and stupid client who gives a slow and disconnected case history.
    The BEST of the following interviewing methods for you to recommend in such a case in order to ascertain facts is for the caseworker to
    A. ask the client leading questions requiring "yes" or "no" answers
    B. request the client to limit his narration to the essential facts so that the interview can be kept as brief as possible
    C. review the story with the client, patiently asking simple questions
    D. tell the client that unless he is more cooperative he cannot be helped to solve his problem

18.____

19. A recent development in casework interviewing procedure, known as multiple-client interviewing, consists of interviews of the entire family at the same time. However, this may not be an effective casework method in certain situations.
    Of the following, the situation in which the standard individual interview would be preferable is when
    A. family member derive consistent and major gratification from assisting each other in their destructive responses
    B. there is a crucial family conflict to which the members are reacting
    C. the family is overwhelmed by interpersonal anxieties which have not been explored
    D. the worker wants to determine the pattern of family interaction to further his diagnostic understanding

19.____

20. A follow-up interview was arranged for an applicant in order that he could furnish 20.____
certain requested evidence. At this follow-up interview, the applicant still fails
to furnish the necessary evidence.
It would be MOST advisable for you to
   A. advise the applicant that he is now considered ineligible
   B. ask the applicant how soon he can get the necessary evidence and set a
      date for another interview
   C. question the applicant carefully and thoroughly to determine if he has
      misrepresented or falsified any information
   D. set a date for another interview and tell the applicant to get the necessary
      evidence by that time

## KEY (CORRECT ANSWERS)

| | | | |
|---|---|---|---|
| 1. | A | 11. | A |
| 2. | D | 12. | A |
| 3. | B | 13. | D |
| 4. | A | 14. | A |
| 5. | D | 15. | C |
| 6. | C | 16. | B |
| 7. | D | 17. | D |
| 8. | D | 18. | C |
| 9. | A | 19. | A |
| 10. | A | 20. | B |

# TEST 2

DIRECTIONS: Each question or incomplete statement is followed by several suggested answers or completions. Select the one that BEST answers the question or completes the statement. *PRINT THE LETTER OF THE CORRECT ANSWER IN THE SPACE AT THE RIGHT.*

1. In interviewing, the practice of anticipating an applicant's answers to questions is generally
    A. *desirable*, because it is effective and economical when it is necessary to interview large numbers of applicants
    B. *desirable*, because many applicants have language difficulties
    C. *undesirable*, because it is the inalienable right of every person to answer as he sees fit
    D. *undesirable*, because applicants may tend to agree with the answer proposed by the interviewer even when the answer is not entirely correct

    1.____

2. When an initial interview is being conducted, one way of starting is to explain the purpose of the interview to the applicant.
    The practice of starting the interview with such an explanation is generally
    A. *desirable*, because the applicant can then understand why the interview is necessary and what will be accomplished by it
    B. *desirable*, because it creates the rapport which is necessary to successful interviewing
    C. *undesirable*, because time will be saved by starting directly with the questions which must be asked
    D. *undesirable*, because the interviewer should have the choice of starting an interview in any manner he prefers

    2.____

3. For you to use responses such as "That's interesting," "Uh-huh," and "Good" during an interview with a patient is
    A. *desirable*, because they indicate that the investigator is attentive
    B. *undesirable*, because they are meaningless to the patient
    C. *desirable*, because the investigator is not supposed to talk excessively
    D. *undesirable*, because they tend to encourage the patient to speak freely

    3.____

4. During the course of a routine interview, the BEST tone of voice for an interviewer to use is
    A. authoritative      B. uncertain
    C. formal             D. conversational

    4.____

5. It is recommended that interviews which inquire into the personal background of an individual should be held in private.
    The BEST reason for this practice is that privacy
    A. allows the individual to talk freely about the details of his background
    B. induces contemplative thought on the part of the interviewed individual
    C. prevents any interruptions by departmental personnel during the interview
    D. most closely resembles the atmosphere of the individual's personal life

    5.____

6. Assume that you are interviewing a patient to determine whether he has any savings accounts.
   To obtain this information, the MOST effective way to phrase your question would be:
   A. "You don't have any savings, do you?"
   B. "At which bank do you have a savings account?"
   C. "Do you have a savings account?"
   D. "May I assume that you have a savings account?"

7. You are interviewing a patient who is not cooperating to the extent necessary to get all required information. Therefore, you decide to be more forceful in your approach.
   In this situation, such a course of action is
   A. *advisable*, because such a change in approach may help to increase the patient's participation
   B. *advisable*, because you will be using your authority more effectively
   C. *inadvisable*, because you will not be able to change this approach if it doesn't produce results
   D. *inadvisable*, because an aggressive approach generally reduces the validity of the interview

8. You have attempted to interview a patient on two separate occasions, and both attempts were unsuccessful. The patient has been totally uncooperative and you sense a personal hostility toward you.
   Of the following, the BEST way to handle this type of situation would be to
   A. speak to the patient in a courteous manner and ask him to explain exactly what he dislikes about you
   B. inform the patient that you will not allow personality conflicts to disrupt the interview
   C. make no further attempt to interview the patient and recommend that he be billed in full
   D. discuss the problem with your supervisor and suggest that another investigator be assigned to try to interview the patient

9. At the beginning of an interview, a patient with normal vision tells you that he is reluctant to discuss his finances. You realize that it will be necessary in this case to ask detailed questions about his net income.
   When you begin this line of questioning, of the following, the LEAST important aspect you should consider is your
   A. precise wording of the question    B. manner of questioning
   C. tone of voice                       D. facial expressions

10. A caseworker under your supervision has been assigned the task of interviewing a man who is applying for foster home placement for his two children. The caseworker seeks your advice as to how to question this man, stating that she finds the applicant to be a timid and self-conscious person who seems torn between the necessity of having to answer the worker's questions truthfully and the effect he thinks his answers will have on his application.

Of the following, the BEST method for the caseworker to use in order to determine the essential facts in this case is to
- A. assure the applicant that he need not worry since the majority of applications for foster home placement are approved
- B. delay the applicant's narration of the facts important to the case until his embarrassment and fears have been overcome
- C. ignore the statements made by the applicant and obtain all the required information from his friends and relatives
- D. inform the applicant that all statements made by him will be verified and are subject to the law governing perjury

11. Assume that a worker is interviewing a boy in his assigned group in order to help him find a job.
    At the BEGINNING of the interview, the worker should
    - A. suggest a possible job for the youth
    - B. refer the youth to an employment agency
    - C. discuss the youth's work history and skills with him
    - D. refer the youth to the manpower and career development agency

12. As part of the investigation to locate an absent father, you make a field visit to interview one of the father's friends. Before beginning the interview, you identify yourself to the friend and show him your official identification.
    For you to do this is, generally,
    - A. *good practice*, because the friend will have proof that you are authorized to make such confidential investigations
    - B. *poor practice*, because the friend may not answer your questions when he knows why you are interviewing him
    - C. *good practice*, because your supervisor can confirm from the friend that you actually made the interview
    - D. *poor practice*, because the friend may warn the absent father that your agency is looking for him

13. You are interviewing a client in his home as part of your investigation of an anonymous complaint that he has been receiving Medicaid fraudulently. During the interview, the client frequently interrupts your questions to discuss the hardships of his life and the bitterness he feels about his medical condition.
    Of the following, the BEST way for you to deal with these discussions is to
    - A. cut them off abruptly, since the client is probably just trying to avoid answering your questions
    - B. listen patiently, since these discussions may be helpful to the client and may give you information for your investigation
    - C. remind the client that you are investigating a complaint against him and he must answer directly
    - D. seek to gain the client's confidence by discussing any personal or medical problems which you yourself may have

14. While interviewing an absent father to determine his ability to pay child support, you realize that his answers to some of your questions contradict his answers to other questions.
    Of the following, the BEST way for you to try to get accurate information from the father is to
    A. confront him with his contradictory answers and demand an explanation from him
    B. use your best judgment as to which of his answers are accurate and question him accordingly
    C. tell him that he has misunderstood your questions and that he must clarify his answers
    D. ask him the same questions in different words and follow up his answer with related questions

14.____

15. Assume that an applicant, obviously under a great deal of stress, talks continuously and rambles, making it difficult for you to determine the exact problem and her need.
    In order to make the interview more successful, it would be BEST for you to
    A. interrupt the applicant and ask her specific questions in order to get the information you need
    B. tell the applicant that her rambling may be a basic cause of her problem
    C. let the applicant continue talking as long as she wishes
    D. ask the applicant to get to the point because other people are waiting for you

15.____

16. A worker must be able to interview clients all day and still be able to listen and maintain interest.
    Of the following, it is MOST important for you to show interest in the client because, if you appear interested,
    A. the client is more likely to appreciate your professional status
    B. the client is more likely to disclose a greater amount of information
    C. the client is less likely to tell lie
    D. you are more likely to gain your supervisor's approval

16.____

17. When you are interviewing clients, it is important to notice and record how they say what they say—angrily, nervously, or with "body English"—because these signs may
    A. tell you that the client's words are the opposite of what the client feels and you may need to dig to find out what those feeling are
    B. be the prelude to violent behavior which no aide is prepared to handle
    C. show that the client does not really deserve serious consideration
    D. be important later should you be asked to defend what you did for the client

17.____

18. The patient you are interviewing is reticent and guarded in responding to your questions. He is not providing the information needed to complete his application for medical assistance.
    In this situation, the one of the following which is the MOST appropriate course of action for you to take FIRST is to

18.____

A. end the interview and ask him to contact you when he is ready to answer your questions
B. advise the patient that you cannot end the interview until he has provided all the information you need to complete the application
C. emphasize to the patient the importance of the questions and the need to answer them in order to complete the application
D. advise the patient that if he answers your questions the interview will be easier for both of you

19. At the end of an interview with a patient, he describes a problem he is having with his teenage son, who is often truant and may be using narcotics. The patient asks you for advice in handling his son.
Of the following, the MOST appropriate action for you to take is to
    A. make an appointment to see the patient and his son together
    B. give the patient a list of drug counseling programs to which he may refer his son
    C. suggest to the patient that his immediate concern should be his own hospitalization rather than his son's problem
    D. tell the patient that you are not qualified to assist him but will attempt to find out who can

20. A MOST appropriate condition in the use of direct questions to obtain personal data in an interview is that, whenever possible,
    A. the direct questions be used only as a means of encouraging the person interviewed to talk about himself
    B. provision be made for recording the information
    C. the direct questions be used only after all other methods have failed
    D. the person being interviewed understands the reason for requesting the information

## KEY (CORRECT ANSWERS)

| | | | |
|---|---|---|---|
| 1. | D | 11. | C |
| 2. | A | 12. | A |
| 3. | A | 13. | B |
| 4. | D | 14. | D |
| 5. | A | 15. | A |
| 6. | B | 16. | B |
| 7. | A | 17. | A |
| 8. | D | 18. | C |
| 9. | A | 19. | D |
| 10. | B | 20. | D |

# PREPARING WRITTEN MATERIAL
# EXAMINATION SECTION
# TEST 1

DIRECTIONS: Each of the following sentences may be classified under one of the following four categories:
A. *Faulty* because of incorrect grammar or usage
B. *Faulty* because of incorrect punctuation or spelling
C. *Faulty* because of incorrect capitalization
D. *Correct*

Examine each sentence carefully. Then, in the correspondingly numbered space on the right, print the capital letter preceding the option which is the best of the four suggested above.

(All incorrect sentences contain but one type of error. Consider a sentence correct if it contains none of the types of errors mentioned, even though there may be other correct ways of expressing the same thought.

1. They gave the poor man some food when he approached. 1.____
2. I regret the loss caused by the error. 2.____
3. The students have a new teacher for shop mantenance. 3.____
4. They sweared to bring out all the facts. 4.____
5. He decided to open a branch store on 33rd street. 5.____
6. His speed is equal and more than that of a racehorse. 6.____
7. He felt very warm on that Summer day. 7.____
8. He was assisted by his friend, who lives in the next house. 8.____
9. The climate of New York is colder than California. 9.____
10. I shall wait for you on the corner. 10.____
11. Did we see the boy whose the leader? 11.____
12. Being a modest person, John seldom takes about his invention. 12.____
13. The gang is called the smith street boys. 13.____
14. He seen the man break into the store. 14.____

15. We expected to lay still there for quite a while. 15._____
16. He is considered to be the Leader of his organization. 16._____
17. Although He received an invitation, He won't go. 17._____
18. The letter must be here some place. 18._____
19. I thought it to be he. 19._____
20. We expect to remain here for a long time. 20._____
21. The committee was agreed. 21._____
22. Two-thirds of the building are finished. 22._____
23. The water was froze. 23._____
24. Everyone of the salesmen must supply their own car. 24._____
25. Who is the author of Gone With the Wind? 25._____
26. He marched on and declaring that he would never surrender. 26._____
27. Who shall I say called? 27._____
28. Everyone has left but they. 28._____
29. Who did we give the order to? 29._____
30. Send your order in immediately. 30._____
31. I believe I paid the Bill. 31._____
32. I have not met but one person. 32._____
33. Why aren't Tom, and Fred, going to the dance? 33._____
34. What reason is there for him not going? 34._____
35. The seige of Malta was a tremendous event. 35._____
36. I was there yesterday I assure you. 36._____
37. Your ukulele is better than mine. 37._____
38. No one was there only Mary. 38._____

3 (#1)

39. The Capital city of Vermont is Montpelier.   39.____

40. Reggie Jackson may hit the largest amount of home runs this season.   40.____

---

## KEY (CORRECT ANSWERS)

| | | | | | | | |
|---|---|---|---|---|---|---|---|
| 1. | B | 11. | B | 21. | D | 31. | C |
| 2. | D | 12. | D | 22. | A | 32. | A |
| 3. | B | 13. | C | 23. | A | 33. | B |
| 4. | A | 14. | A | 24. | A | 34. | A |
| 5. | C | 15. | A | 25. | B | 35. | B |
| 6. | A | 16. | C | 26. | A | 36. | B |
| 7. | C | 17. | C | 27. | D | 37. | B |
| 8. | D | 18. | A | 28. | D | 38. | A |
| 9. | A | 19. | A | 29. | A | 39. | C |
| 10. | D | 20. | D | 30. | D | 40. | A |

# TEST 2

Questions 1-3.

DIRECTIONS: Questions 1 through 3 each consist of four sentences. Choose the one sentence in each set of four that would be BEST for a formal letter or report. Consider grammar and appropriate usage.

1. A. Most all the work he completed before he become ill.
   B. He completed most of the work before becoming ill.
   C. Prior to him becoming ill his work was mostly completed.
   D. Before he became will most of the work he had completed.

2. A. Being that the report lacked a clearly worded recommendation, it did not matter that it contained enough information.
   B. There was enough information in the report, although it, including the recommendation, were not clearly worded.
   C. Although the report contained enough information, it did not have a clearly worded recommendation.
   D. Though the report did not have a recommendation that was clearly worded, and the information therein contained was enough.

3. A. Having already overlooked the important mistakes, the ones which she found were not as important toward the end of the letter.
   B. Toward the end of the letter she had already overlooked the important mistakes, so that which she had found were not important.
   C. The mistakes which she had already overlooked were not as important as those which near the end of letter she had found.
   D. The mistakes which she found near the end of the letter were not so important as those which she had already overlooked.

Questions 4-5.

DIRECTIONS: Select the correct answer.

4. The unit has exceeded _____ goals and the employees are satisfied with _____ accomplishments.
   A. their; it's    B. it's, it's    C. is, there    D. its, their

5. Research indicates that employees who _____ no opportunity for close social relationships often find their work unsatisfying, and this _____ of satisfaction often reflects itself in low production.
   A. have, lack    B. have, excess    C. has, lack    D. has, excess

## KEY (CORRECT ANSWERS)

1. B
2. C
3. D
4. D
5. A

# TEST 3

DIRECTIONS: Select the choice which BEST expresses the thought and which contains NO errors in grammar or sentence construction.

1. A. She, hearing a signal, the source lamp flashed.
   B. While hearing a signal, the source lamp flashed
   C. In hearing a signal, the source lamp flashed.
   D. As she heard a signal, the source lamp flashed.

   1.____

2. A. Every one of the time records have been initialed in the designated spaces.
   B. All of the time records has been initialed in the designated spaces.
   C. Which one of the time records was initialed in the designated spaces.
   D. The time records all been initialed in the designated spaces.

   2.____

3. A. If there is no one else to answer the phone, you will have to answer it.
   B. You will have to answer it yourself if no one else answers the phone.
   C. If no one else is not around to pick up the phone, you have to do it.
   D. You will have to answer the phone when nobodys here to do it.

   3.____

4. A. Dr. Byrnes not in his office. What could I do for you?
   B. Dr. Byrnes is not in his office. Is there something I can do for you?
   C. Since Dr. Byrnes is not in his office, might there be something I may do for you?
   D. Is there any ways I can assist you since Dr. Brynes is not in his office?

   4.____

5. A. She do not understand how the new console works.
   B. The way the new console works, she doesn't understand.
   C. She doesn't understand how the new console works.
   D. The new console works, so that she doesn't understand.

   5.____

## KEY (CORRECT ANSWERS)

1. D
2. C
3. A
4. B
5. C

# TEST 4

DIRECTIONS: The following questions each consist of a sentence which may or may not be an example of good English usage.

Consider grammar, punctuation, spelling, capitalization, awkwardness, etc.

Examine each sentence and then choose the correct statement about it from the four choices below. If the English usage in the sentence given is better than any of the changes suggested in options B, C, or D, choose option A. (Do not choose an option that will change the meaning of the sentence.)

1. The typist used an extention cord in order to connect her typewriter to the outlet nearest to her desk.
    A. This is an example of acceptable writing.
    B. A period should be placed after the word "cord" and the word "in" should have a capital "I."
    C. A comma should be placed after the word "typewriter."
    D. The word "extention" should be spelled "extension."

2. He would have went to the conference if he had received an invitation.
    A. This is an example of acceptable writing.
    B. The word "went" should be replaced by the word "gone."
    C. The word "had" should be replaced by "would have."
    D. The word "conference" should be spelled "conference."

3. In order to make the report neater, he spent many hours rewriting it.
    A. This is an example of acceptable writing.
    B. The word "more" should be inserted before the word "neater."
    C. There should be a colon after the word "neater."
    D. The word "spent" should be changed to "have spent."

4. His supervisor told him that he should of read the memorandum more carefully.
    A. This is an example of acceptable writing.
    B. The word "memorandum" should be spelled "memorandom."
    C. The word "of" should be replaced by the word "have."
    D. The word "carefully" should be replaced by the word "have."

5. It was decided that two separate reports should be written.
    A. This is an example of acceptable writing.
    B. A comma should be inserted after the word "decided."
    C. The word "be" should be replaced by the word "been."
    D. A colon should be inserted after the word "that."

6. She don't seem to understand that the work must be done as soon as possible.
    A. This is an example of acceptable writing.
    B. The word "doesn't" should replace the word "don't."
    C. The word "why" should replace the word "that."
    D. The word "as" before the word "soon" should be eliminated.

## KEY (CORRECT ANSWERS)

1. D
2. B
3. A
4. C
5. A
6. B

# QUESTIONS & ANSWERS ABOUT AIDS

1. What is AIDS?

   Acquired immune deficiency syndrome (AIDS) is the final and most severe stage of HIV infection. AIDS is a disease in which the body's natural immune system breaks down, leaving it unable to fight off infections. A person with AIDS gets illnesses that are little or no threat to someone with a healthy immune system.

2. What causes AIDS?

   AIDS is caused by a virus called human immunodeficiency virus (HIV).

3. Do all people infected with HIV have AIDS?

   No. It can take years for illness to appear. Most people infected with HIV may have initial flu-like symptoms for a few days, and then go for years without any symptoms. People often do not even know they are infected. Symptoms may then develop, varying in severity from mild to extremely serious. AIDS is the final and most severe stage of HIV infection.

   All people with HIV infection, whether or not it has progressed to AIDS, can pass the virus to others.

4. Is there a cure for AIDS?

   There is still no cure for AIDS, but early diagnosis of HIV infection and medical treatment can help people with HIV infection stay healthy longer by delaying or preventing the onset of AIDS.

## HIV TRANSMISSION

5. How is HIV transmitted?

   HIV is not an easily transmissible virus. HIV is spread by direct contact with infected body fluids, including blood, semen, vaginal secretions, and breast milk. This means that HIV contained in one of these fluids can enter the bloodstream through direct entry into a vein, a break in the skin or mucous linings, such as eyes, mouth, nose, vagina, rectum or urethra. Other body fluids such as urine, saliva, vomitus, etc. do not pose a risk unless visible blood is present. The virus is not transmitted through air, water, food or casual contact such as handshaking, hugging or sharing restrooms, drinking fountains, etc.

6. How infectious is HIV?

   Unlike most viral infections – colds, flu, measles, etc. – HIV is not transmitted through sneezing, coughing, eating or drinking from common utensils or merely being around a person with HIV infection. Casual contact with people with HIV infection does not place others at risk. No cases have ever been found where HIV has been transmitted through casual contact with a household member, relative, co-worker or friend.

7. What behaviors put an individual at risk for HIV infection?

    Behaviors that may put an individual at increased risk (high risk behaviors) for HIV infection include:

    - Sharing injectable drug needles or works with a person infected with HIV or whose HIV status is unknown;
    - Having unprotected anal, oral or vaginal sex (without using a latex condom) with a person infected with HIV or whose HIV status is unknown;
    - Women with HIV infection can also pass the virus to their babies during pregnancy, delivery, and through breastfeeding.

8. Who is at risk for HIV infection?

    Anyone who participates in high risk behaviors can become infected with HIV and may develop AIDS.

9. Why have many homosexual and bisexual men developed AIDS?

    Cases of AIDS among homosexual and bisexual men are linked with sexual contact, particularly anal intercourse and other sexual practices that result in semen-to-blood or blood-to-blood contact. Anyone who has anal sex with a partner infected with HIV or with a partner whose HIV status is unknown, is at increased risk for HIV infection, whether the person is homosexual or heterosexual.

10. Why is IV drug use a high risk behavior for HIV infection?

    IV drug users often share needles, syringes, cotton, cookers, water, and other equipment used for injecting drugs. Small amounts of blood from a person infected with HIV may remain on the equipment and may be injected into the bloodstream of the next person who uses the equipment. Also, used needles and works can be packaged as new and sold on the street.

    Any needle-sharing with a person infected with HIV is a high risk behavior. This includes needles used for IV drug use, skin popping, intramuscular injection, such as steroids, piercing and tattooing.

11. Why have many persons with hemophilia become infected with HIV?

    People with hemophilia receive frequent transfusions of blood plasma concentrates that must be prepared from hundreds to thousands of blood donations. Cases of AIDS among persons with hemophilia have been linked with receipt of blood products from donors infected with HIV prior to the implementation of heat treatment of plasma products in 1984 and the screening of blood donations for HIV antibodies in mid-1985.

12. What is the risk of getting HIV from a blood transfusion?

    The risk of HIV infection through a blood transfusion is extremely remote and has been significantly reduced through health history screening and mandatory HIV antibody testing of blood donations which began in May 1985 in New York State. Research studies indicate that the HIV antibody test is highly effective in eliminating blood that may be infected with HIV from the donor pool.

    All people with HIV, AIDS, or those whose behavior has placed them at risk for HIV infection are asked to refrain from donating blood. All blood units that test positive for HIV antibodies are removed from the transfusion pool.

13. Is there a danger of becoming infected with HIV from donating blood?

    No. Blood banks and other blood collection centers use sterile equipment and disposable needles. The need for blood is always acute, and people who do not engage in high risk behavior are urged to continue to donate blood as they have in the past.

14. How do women become infected with HIV?

    Women become infected by engaging in unprotected sex or by sharing injectable drug needles and works with an infected person. While more than 50 percent of women with AIDS have used IV drugs, the fastest growing number of cases is among female sex partners of IV drug users. Women who have sex with other women are also at risk for HIV infection because the virus can be transmitted by infected vaginal secretions and menstrual blood.

15. How do adolescents become infected with HIV?

    Adolescence can be a time of sexual and drug experimentation. Many teens may also feel peer pressure regarding sex and drug use. As with any individual, adolescents who participate in unprotected sex and needle sharing activity put themselves at risk for becoming HIV infected. "Getting high" on alcohol, crack cocaine, and other non-injectable drugs can impair one's ability to make responsible decisions about sex or injecting drug use, tattooing and piercing (i.e., nose, ears, etc.).

16. Is HIV passed by kissing?

    Trace amounts of HIV have been found in the saliva of some people with AIDS, but there are no cases of HIV infection that are known or suspected of being transmitted by kissing. Kissing that involves exchange of saliva (French kissing or deep kissing) may involve some risk. Casual kissing, such as between parents and children, has not transmitted HIV.

17. Can HIV be transmitted through anal sex?

    Yes. The lining of the rectum is thin, easily torn, and is often injured during anal intercourse. Bacteria and viruses, such as HIV, can easily enter the bloodstream through bruised tissue. For this reason, unprotected anal sex is the most risky sexual behavior for spreading HIV from an infected person to their partner(s). While latex condoms can provide some protection, their failure rate during anal sex is greater than that for vaginal and oral sex. (See Question 24). Therefore, even anal six with a condom is risky.

18. Can HIV be transmitted through vaginal sex?

    Yes. A growing number of women have become infected through vaginal intercourse with males who are HIV infected. HIV has been found in vaginal secretions and menstrual blood can be transmitted to male partners, particularly if there is a sore or cut on the penis. HIV can also be transmitted from female to female through shared sex toys.

19. Why is HIV more easily transmitted from men to women during vaginal intercourse?

    HIV is more highly concentrated in semen than in vaginal secretions. Since the vagina is lined with a mucous membrane, it may be easier for HIV to enter the body. Women are also likely to have longer exposure to the virus because semen is retained in the vagina following intercourse.

20. Can HIV be transmitted through oral/genital sex?

    Yes. A few people have become infected with HIV by having oral sex with a partner infected with HIV. Since the mouth is lined with mucous membrane, contact with infectious blood, semen, or vaginal secretions may make it easier for HIV to enter the body. The presence of cuts such as those caused by toothbrushing, lesions (canker sores, blisters, etc.) or other open areas in or around the mouth may further increase the risk.

    Use of a latex condom for oral sex provides the best protection against the transmission of the virus. Latex dental dams (latex material cut in squares) may provide some protection, but they have not been studied to determine their effectiveness. Additionally, no studies have been conducted on plastic wrap to prove its effectiveness as a barrier against HIV. However, plastic wrap is a microscopically porous substance which may let HIV pass through.

21. Does sexual contact with many partners increase the risk of HIV infection?

    Yes. Unprotected sex with many partners increases the risk of coming into contact with someone who is infected with HIV, as well as other sexually transmitted diseases, such as syphilis, gonorrhea, and herpes.

22. Can sexual prostitution spread HIV?

    Yes. If either the sex worker or the client is infected with HIV, the virus may be passed to the uninfected person through unprotected sex. Anyone who engages in anal, oral or vaginal sex without using a latex condom is at increased risk of contracting HIV and other sexually transmitted diseases.

23. Can other sexually transmissible diseases increase the risk of HIV?

    Yes. Any sore caused by a sexually transmitted disease such as herpes, gonorrhea or syphilis could make it easier for HIV to enter the bloodstream during sexual contact. Studies show higher rates of HIV infection among men and women who have syphilis.

24. Can use of a latex condom during sex reduce the risk of HIV infection?

    Yes. Use of a latex condom during sex can reduce the risk of HIV infection since it minimizes direct contact with semen, blood, and vaginal secretions (fluids known to carry the virus). Since condoms are not failsafe, people should not relay on them as their only defense against HIV. Additional protection can also be provided by using a spermicide in case the condom leaks or slips. Condoms have an approximate 10% failure rate for vaginal and oral sex and an approximate 26% failure rate for anal sex. Failure rates may be due to improper storage, handling or use or improper quality control by the manufacturer. It is safest to avoid anal, oral or vaginal sex unless you know for certain your partner is not infected.

    (Natural or lambskin condoms are not effective protection against HIV because they allow the virus to pass through.)

25. Can use of a diaphragm and spermicide reduce the risk of HIV infection?

    Although there are no human studies, laboratory and animal studies suggest that a diaphragm with a spermicide may reduce the risk of HIV infection. A spermicidal jelly, or cream, should be applied to the rim and side of the diaphragm covering the cervix. Additional spermicide inserted directly into the vagina is also recommended. A diaphragm and vaginal spermicide should only be used by a woman whenever latex condom use cannot be negotiated with a male partner.

26. Can use of spermicides alone reduce the risk of HIV infection?

    The extent to which spermicides alone may provide protection has not been well documented. However, spermicides applied within the vagina may provide protection against the virus contained in semen. This method of protection should only be used as the very last resort. Latex condoms with spermicide provide the most protection against HIV infection while use of a diaphragm with a spermicide offers some protection to the female partner.

27. Can birth control pills or douching after sex prevent HIV infection?

    No. Birth control pills provide no protection against HIV. Douching is also ineffective because sperm enter the cervical canal almost immediately after ejaculation. Latex condoms (which prevent direct contact with semen, blood, and vaginal secretions) with spermicide have been shown to be most effective in reducing the risk of HIV transmission during sexual intercourse.

28. How can people reduce their risk of getting HIV through sexual contact?

   All sexually active people should avoid unprotected sex which involves direct contact with body fluids (semen, vaginal secretions, blood) unless they know for certain their partner is not infected with HIV. Use of a latex condom with a spermicide containing nonoxynol-9 during vaginal and anal sex and a dry latex condom during oral sex reduces the risk of direct contact with infected body fluids. Extra protection can be provided by also using vaginal spermicides.

29. Can a person with no symptoms transmit HIV?

   Yes. Initially, most people with HIV infection have no symptoms and are not even aware they are infected. Any person infected with HIV may transmit the virus to another person through unprotected sexual contact or sharing needles or drug injection equipment.

30. Can you get infected by being in the same house with a person with HIV infection or AIDS?

   Many studies have shown that transmission of HIV through casual contact does not occur, even among family members living in the same house.

31. Can you get infected by drinking from the same glass or eating from the same dishes as a person with HIV infection or AIDS?

   More than ten years of experience shows that HIV is not transmitted in households where people may drink or eat from common dishes or utensils.

32. Can you get HIV infection from public toilets, drinking fountains, restaurants, telephones, or public transportation?

   HIV is not transmitted through the air, food, or water, or by touching any object handled, touched, or breathed on by a person infected with HIV.

33. Can you get HIV by touching someone who has it?

   There is no evidence that HIV is spread through any form of casual contact, including handshaking, bumping together in crowds, contact sports or even casual kissing.

34. Can HIV be spread by swimming pools or hot tubs?

   There are no cases of HIV transmitted through swimming pools or hot tubs. The virus would be killed by the normal levels of chlorine used to disinfect public swimming pools, saunas, or hot tubs.

35. Can you get HIV from using someone's razor or toothbrush?

   To date, no cases of HIV infection are linked with sharing razors or toothbrushes. However, since toothbrushes and razors can cause cuts and scrapes, it is wise to avoid sharing personal items that may come into contact with another person's blood.

36. Can you get HIV from ear piercing or tattoo needles?

    So far, no AIDS cases have been linked with any body part piercing or tattooing. However, to guard against possible infection, all needles or equipment used for these procedures should be sterilized between each use.

37. Can you get HIV infection or AIDS from a co-worker?

    No. HIV is not transmitted through casual contact. No cases of AIDS have developed among casual friends or co-workers of people infected with HIV. There is no evidence that being around someone with HIV or AIDS, even for an extended period of time, puts you at risk.

38. What is the risk of living in a neighborhood that has a hospital or home for people with HIV infection or AIDS?

    None, since HIV is not transmitted through the air or through any kind of casual contact.

39. Can mosquitoes transmit HIV?

    Studies have shown there is no evidence that mosquitoes, other insects or rodents play any role in the transmission of HIV to humans.

40. Can you get HIV from dental instruments?

    There has been one report linking a dentist who had AIDS with the transmission of HIV to five of his patients. However, it is unclear how these cases occurred. The potential for transmission in a dental setting is remote. Standard disinfection and sterilization procedures used for cleaning dental equipment and instruments are effective against HIV, hepatitis B, and other blood-borne diseases.

41. What should I do if I'm concerned about getting HIV infection from a visit to the doctor, dentist or other health professional?

    Getting HIV infection or other blood-borne diseases from your doctor, dentist or other health care professionals is extremely unlikely. For their protection, as well as yours, health care workers are required to use infection control measures that minimize direct exposure to patients' or workers' blood. (See Question 87b.)

    If you have questions about how infection control measures are followed in the office of your health provider, you should ask for this information. Most professionals will be very willing to discuss this with you.

42. Are health care workers or other occupational groups at increased risk for HIV infection?

    In the U.S., it is estimated that on a yearly basis more than a million punctures and other occupational exposures occur in health care settings. Of these exposures, 2% or more than 20,000 are likely to be contaminated with HIV.

This information demonstrates the need for health care workers and other occupational groups who come in contact with body fluids to strictly follow safety guidelines to prevent direct exposure to potentially infectious body fluids during patient care.

## AIDS INCIDENCE

Statistics refer to reported cases of AIDS, not the number of individuals infected with HIV.

43. How many cases of AIDS have occurred so far?

    In the U.S., there have been more than 1.2 million cases of AIDS reported to the Centers for Disease Control. For an update of reported AIDS cases nationally, contact the National AIDS Hotline at 1-800-343-AIDS.

44. What is the geographic distribution of AIDS cases?

    21% of the AIDS cases reported in the U.S. were reported to CDC from New York State and 19% from California. AIDS cases have been reported from the fifty states, the District of Columbia, Puerto Rico, and more than 140 other countries.

45. How many children have developed AIDS?

    Approximately 3,470 children under 13 years of age have developed AIDS; about 27% of these children live in New York State.

46. What is the racial/ethnic breakdown of people with AIDS?

    | United States | White | Black | Hispanic | *Other |
    |---|---|---|---|---|
    | Total Population | 76% | 12% | 8% | 4% |
    | AIDS Cases | 54% | 29% | 16% | .8% |
    | New York State | White | Black | Hispanic | *Other |
    | Total Population | 69% | 14% | 12% | 4.2% |
    | AIDS Cases | 36% | 36% | 27% | .6% |

    (*Other = Asian/Pacific Islander, American Indian, Eskimo and Aleut)

47. How many Americans are infected with HIV?

    The federal government estimates that approximately one million Americans are infected with the virus, and may develop AIDS in the future.

48. Is AIDS occurring only in our country?

    AIDS is a worldwide problem. Most countries have reported AIDS cases, including those in North America, South America, Europe, Africa, the Caribbean, South America, Australia, the Middle East and Asia.

49. Do AIDS cases in other countries show the same risk factors as here?

    In general, the same risk factors – unprotected sex and sharing drug injection equipment – are associated with AIDS everywhere. However, in some foreign countries, transfusions and unsterile medical procedures, such as re-using needles and other invasive equipment, may also spread HIV infection from patient to patient. Studies are underway to gain a better understanding of the similarities and differences of AIDS cases in the U.S. and other countries.

**DIAGNOSIS AND TREATMENT**

50. Is there a blood test for AIDS?

    No. However, the HIV antibody test can detect antibodies (substances produced in the blood to fight disease organisms) to HIV, the virus that causes AIDS. Presence of these antibodies in the bloodstream means that a person is infected with the virus. A positive test does not mean a person has AIDS. There are other laboratory tests that can detect immune system damage associated with HIV infection and AIDS.

51. How soon after becoming infected with HIV do antibodies develop?

    Antibodies develop almost immediately in response to the virus. Most people infected with HIV develop antibodies in levels high enough to be detected by the HIV antibody test within a few weeks, but it may take up to 6 months or more. All people infected with HIV, whether or not they have developed detectable levels of antibodies, can transmit the virus to others through unprotected sexual contact or needle-sharing. A mother infected with HIV can also transmit the virus to her baby during pregnancy, delivery, or by breastfeeding.

52. Should people wait until they have symptoms before they get tested?

    No. People who are concerned that they may be infected with HIV should seek counseling and testing as soon as possible after exposure. The counselor will explain the test and suggest ways to reduce further risk of HIV infection. If the infection has been very recent, and the HIV antibody test result is negative, the HIV counselor may suggest retesting within three months to ensure that antibodies have developed in levels high enough to be detected by the test. The earlier HIV infection is detected, the sooner medical treatment can begin which can help people stay healthy longer.

53. Where can people concerned about HIV and AIDS get antibody testing?

    The Health Department operates sites that offer free HIV counseling and testing for people who wish to know if they are infected. People receive counseling about testing options, what the test results mean, and actions they may take to minimize further exposure to the virus or potential transmission to others. Many private physicians and clinics, such as STD (sexually transmitted disease) clinics, drug treatment programs, and community health centers, also provide HIV counseling and testing. All HIV-related information is confidential and protected by law.

For information, call 1-800-872-2777, 1-800-541-AIDS, 1-800-233-SIDA (Spanish-speaking operators), your personal physician, or the nearest HIV counseling/testing program.

54. What are the early symptoms of HIV infection?

Many people infected with HIV have no symptoms at all and may be unaware that they carry the virus. Some people may develop mild, temporary flu-like symptoms that disappear after a few days or weeks following infection. Other may have persistent swollen glands. All people with HIV infection, whether or not they have any symptoms, can transmit the virus to others through unprotected sexual contact or needle-sharing. Women infected with HIV can also transmit the virus to their babies during pregnancy, delivery, or by breastfeeding.

55. What are the symptoms of advancing HIV disease and AIDS?

Many of the symptoms of advancing HIV disease are similar to other health problems not related to HIV. The following symptoms should prompt a medical evaluation to determine the cause, appropriate treatment and whether they are HIV-related. Symptoms may include:

- Extreme tiredness, sometimes combined with headache, dizziness, or lightheadedness;
- swollen glands in the neck, armpits or groin;
- continued fever or night sweats;
- weight loss of more than 10 pounds not due to dieting or increased physical activity;
- purple or discolored growths on the skin or the mucous membranes (inside the mouth, anus or nasal passages);
- heavy, continual dry cough that is not from smoking or that has lasted too long to be a cold or flu;
- progressive shortness of breath;
- continuing bouts of diarrhea;
- thrush, a thick whitish coating on the tongue or in the throat which may be accompanied by a sore throat;
- recurring vaginal yeast infections;
- unexplained bleeding from any body opening or from growths on the skin or mucous membranes;
- bruising more easily than usual;
- forgetfulness, confusion, disorientation and other signs of mental deterioration.

56. When does HIV infection become AIDS?

AIDS is the last stage in the disease progression resulting from HIV infection. A person is diagnosed as having AIDS when he or she develops one or more of the opportunistic diseases associated with HIV infection. These diseases include a number of unusual infections and cancers, as well as debilitating illnesses resulting in severe weight loss, or wasting and/or affecting the brain and nervous system. Two of the most common opportunistic infections include pneumocystis carinii pneumonia (PCP), and Kaposi's sarcoma (KS), a cancer that appears as red or purplish areas on the skin.

57. How is HIV infection treated?

    Certain drugs have been found to help control the virus and to prevent or delay the onset of AIDS. Medical research shows that the earlier these drugs are given, the more likely it is that a person infected with HIV will stay healthy longer. Some of the drugs are antivirals that attack the virus and help prevent it from multiplying inside the body. Examples of these include zidovudine (ZDV), often called AZT, dideoxyinosine (ddI) and dideoxycytidine (ddC). Other drugs are used to treat the cancers and infections that may affect people with HIV infection.

58. Why is it important for someone with HIV infection to get medical care?

    a.  Initial Evaluation and Treatment: It is important for a person infected with HIV to seek medical care as soon as possible after diagnosis so that tests for other infections, such as tuberculosis (TB) and sexually transmitted diseases (STD's) can be done and medical treatment provided as needed. The physician will also determine the extent of damage to the patient's immune system, if any, and prescribe medications to slow the progress of HIV disease. If a woman is pregnant or recently had a baby, the physician can provide both mother and child appropriate medical care. The progression of HIV infection in young children is frequently different from that in adults; some children become sick more quickly. It is important that children with HIV infection received medical care at an early age.

    b.  Regular Evaluation and Treatment: Regular medical evaluation and treatment allows the physician to monitor the patient's immune system and overall health status. The physician can also offer the patient information about new medical treatments, as well as reinforce the benefits of good health practices.

59. What is the connection between TB and HIV?

    Since 1986 there has been a resurgence of tuberculosis (TB) in the United States. This increase is largely due to TB occurring in persons with HIV infection.

    TB is one of the many diseases that is controlled by the immune system. Most people who come in contact with TB organisms do not get sick because the organisms remain inactive. However, if a person's immune system is weakened, as it is with someone who has HIV infection, it is more likely that the person will develop active TB disease. General symptoms of TB are similar to those of other HIV-related diseases. These include: weakness, feeling sick, weight loss, fever, and night sweats. Therefore, it is very important for individuals with HIV infection to get tested for TB. Active TB can be prevented through medication which is taken before symptoms develop.

60. How can people with HIV infection learn about experimental treatments?

    The AIDS Clinical Trials Information Service acts as a central source of information on many federally and privately sponsored clinical trials for people with HIV infection and AIDS. Call 1-800-TRIALS-A for the latest information on HIV and AIDS clinical trials.

The American Foundation for AIDS Research (AmFAR) produces and distributes a directory of all clinical HIV drug trials in New York State (New York State Director of Clinical Trials). For information on how to obtain the director, call 212-682-7440.

Additional information for clinical trials in New York, New Jersey, Connecticut, and Philadelphia can be obtained from the AIDS Institute Experimental Treatments Hotline at 212-613-4348. The hotline provides a computerized database of current experimental treatments and information for individualized searches based on your $T_4$ cell count.

61. Where can people with HIV or AIDS get medical care?

    People with HIV infection or AIDS are treated in hospitals, physician's offices, clinics, or other health care settings, just like any other patient. These patients do not pose a significant risk to other patients or health care workers who follow recommended safety precautions. People who need referral to physicians and health facilities may contact the nearest AIDS hotline or HIV counseling and testing program.

62. Do some hospitals specialize in AIDS care?

    The State Health Department has designated a number of hospitals as AIDS Care Centers, because they have specialized care programs for people with HIV infection and AIDS. These hospitals are generally involved in HIV-related research programs. AIDS Centers are required to coordinate the full range of medical services needed by patients with HIV and AIDS, including inpatient and outpatient care, home health care, dentistry, and psychosocial counseling. Some AIDS Centers have special units to care for women, children, and adolescents with HIV and AIDS.

63. Are there special nursing homes for people with HIV infection or AIDS?

    There is a growing need for nursing home care for patients with HIV infection or AIDS, particularly for those who are homeless or who have no family support system. To fill this need, the State Health Department continues to encourage the development of specialized HIV/AIDS nursing homes that provide medical and other specialized services.

64. Who pays for treatment of people with HIV infection and AIDS?

    Care for patients with HIV infection and AIDS is paid for by the same means as all medical care: the government (Medicaid and Medicare), private insurance companies and individuals. Most group health insurance plans cover HIV and AIDS medical treatment, although most have maximum allowances. The cost of care for a patient with symptomatic HIV infection or AIDS can be as much as $50,000 per year.

    All of the HIV treatment drugs require a doctor's prescription. Many of the drugs are expensive, but there are programs which pay for the drugs if persons have no private insurance coverage or other resources. The State Medicaid Program covers the drugs for Medicaid-eligible persons. The State AIDS Drug Assistance Program (ADAP) offers free drugs for other people who need help paying for medications. For further information, call: 1-800-542-AIDS.

65. Can people with HIV infection or AIDS be denied health care coverage?

    Some insurance companies require new applicants for health insurance policies to undergo an HIV antibody test. If the test is positive, the courts have ruled that insurance companies may deny coverage or increase the premiums.

66. Does anyone ever survive AIDS?

    Some people with AIDS are still alive many years after diagnosis. New treatments show promise of extending the life expectancy of people with HIV and AIDS. Since there is still no cure that will rid the body of the virus, we don't know how long people with AIDS can live.

67. Is there a vaccine to prevent AIDS?

    There is currently no vaccine to protect a person from HIV or AIDS. Researchers in the U.S. and other countries are actively working to develop a vaccine. Scientists report that this may be difficult because the virus can alter its form in the human body.

## AIDS AMONG CHILDREN AND ADOLESCENTS

68. How do children get HIV infection and AIDS?

    The majority of children infected with HIV got the virus from their infected mothers, presumably through blood exchange in the uterus or during birth. A mother infected with the virus can transmit it to her baby even if she has no symptoms of HIV infection or AIDS. It is also possible for her to pass the virus to her infant through breast milk. A few children became infected from blood transfusions prior to the screening of the blood supply in mid-1985.

69. What is the risk of a baby becoming HIV infected if its mother is infected?

    Studies indicate that approximately 20-40 percent of babies born to mothers infected with HIV will become infected. A mother with HIV infection can transmit the virus even if she herself has no symptoms.

70. Can babies get HIV infection from breast milk?

    Yes. HIV has been detected in breast milk. There have been a few cases of AIDS which have been transmitted to an infant through mother's milk. Any woman who is infected with HIV is advised to refrain from nursing as a precautionary measure.

71. Why is it important for women who are planning a pregnancy to be tested for HIV?

    All women of child-bearing age should be tested for HIV prior to pregnancy, if they or their partner have engaged in high risk behavior. If a woman is infected, she can pass the virus to her child. Women are at risk for HIV infection if they have ever shared needles or works or had unprotected sex with individuals whose HIV status was unknown.

72. Should a parent or guardian inform their child's physician if the child is HIV positive?

    Yes. The child's parent or guardian should inform the child's physician about the child's positive HIV status in order for the physician to provide appropriate medical care and monitoring.

73. Should a child infected with HIV receive routine childhood immunizations?

    Yes. Immunizations are critical to the health of all children, including those infected with HIV. Infants and children infected with HIV lose vaccine immunity as HIV infection progresses. Therefore, it is important to seek medical care for the child as soon as possible after exposure to any childhood disease, even if the child has been previously vaccinated. Remember to tell the physician your child is HIV positive so appropriate care can be provided.

74. If a child is infected with HIV, can he/she infect another child?

    None of the identified cases of HIV infection in the United States is known or suspected to have been transmitted from one child to another in the home, school, day care or foster care setting. Even baby twins, one infected and one not, sharing nipples, toys, food, bed, and playpen, have not passed the virus between them.

75. What risk does interacting with siblings or other children pose to a child infected with HIV?

    A child whose immune system is damaged by HIV is highly susceptible to infections from siblings at home or other children in a school or day care setting. Assessing the risk of attending school for an immunosuppressed child is best done by the child's physician who is aware of the child's immune status.

76. What is the State's recommendation on children with HIV infection or AIDS attending schools?

    In general, students or children with AIDS or HIV infection should be allowed to attend school and classes, if physically able. School officials do not have the right to exclude a student or teacher infected with HIV from school or demand that the HIV status or AIDS diagnosis of a child, parent, or teacher be revealed.

    Decisions regarding the type of educational setting for children with HIV infection or AIDS should be based on the behavior, neurologic development, and physical condition of the child. These evaluations should be made on a confidential basis to protect the child against potential discrimination. The appropriate decision makers would include the child's parent or guardian, and physician, with consultant from public health personnel and school officials, if necessary.

77. Is there a risk of spreading HIV infection to others by teachers, cooks, or other school personnel who may be infected with HIV or AIDS?

    No. HIV is not spread through air, food, water, or any form of casual contact. There are no cases of HIV infection reported anywhere that are known or suspected of being transmitted through food preparation, use of common toilets or drinking fountains, or merely having long-term casual contact with a person with HIV or AIDS.

78. Suppose my child became a playmate of a child with HIV infection or AIDS?

    Casual contact, even over a long period of time, is not dangerous. In household studies, no child living with a person with HIV or AIDS has been known to contract the virus through day-to-day activities or contact.

79. What if my child is in a classroom with a child who is infected with HIV who vomited or had diarrhea?

    Care should be taken to minimize contact with bodily secretions or excretions from any ill person. People cleaning up such secretions are advised to wear gloves and to use a solution of household bleach and water (¼ bleach to a gallon of water) as a disinfectant. While these precautions are recommended, it should be noted that no cases of HIV infection have ever been linked with exposure to urine, saliva, vomit, or feces. The body fluids linked with HIV transmission are blood, semen, vaginal secretions, and breast milk.

80. Since HIV is transmitted through blood contact, could a child get it through a schoolyard fight or during a contact sport like football?

    It is highly unlikely that transmission could occur in this manner. The external contact with blood that might occur in a sports injury is very different from direct entry of blood into the bloodstream which occurs from sharing injectable drug needles or works.

81. Why is it important that adolescents understand how HIV is transmitted?

    Although less than 1% of all reported AIDS cases in the U.S. are among adolescents, nearly 20% of reported AIDS cases are among persons age 20-29. It is unlikely that many of these persons were infected during adolescence.

    Adolescence is a time of learning and experimenting. Sexual and drug experimentation, combined with feelings of invulnerability, contribute to adolescents' risk of HIV infection. Unless teens are informed about the consequences of these risky behavior patterns and are offered options, unsafe sex and drug use activities may continue into adulthood.

82. How can I inform my child about HIV and AIDS?

    It is important for you to learn the facts about HIV and AIDS before you discuss this subject with your child. Basic information related to HIV and AIDS are available from a variety of sources, such as health departments, clinics, physicians, libraries, and AIDS-related community organizations.

Materials specifically directed toward parents are available from the National AIDS Information Clearinghouse (1-800-458-5231).

It's best to start discussing the issues with your child before he/she is sexually active or involved in possible drug experimentation. This will help establish open lines of communication. Look for opportunities to discuss AIDS-related issues with your child. Use radio, TV and newspaper articles to start a conversation or ask your child what AIDS-related information he/she is learning in school.

## PREVENTING THE SPREAD OF HIV

83. What is being done to prevent the spread of HIV?

    a. Education: Since there is still no cure or vaccine for HIV infection or AIDS, education is the most effective preventive measure. Educational campaigns are directed to the general public and those who engage in high risk behavior, encouraging them to avoid or discontinue any practices which have been linked with the possible spread of HIV infection or AIDS.

    All sexually active men and women are advised to refrain from unprotected sexual contact unless they know for sure their partner is not infected. Use of latex condoms with nonoxynol-9 during anal, oral, or vaginal sex can reduce direct exposure to body fluids, and the risk of HIV infection and other sexually transmitted diseases. Men and women who have had or currently have sexual contact with a number of partners or with a single partner whose HIV status is unknown are advised to obtain HIV counseling and testing to determine if they have been infected with HIV. This will allow for risk reduction counseling and early treatment if a person is infected.

    Injecting drug users are urged not to share needles or other drug injection equipment and to enter drug treatment programs to become drug free. Injecting drug users should also seek HIV antibody testing. Until they know from their HIV antibody test result that they are not infected, they should use latex condoms with spermicide containing nonoxynol-9 to reduce the possibility of spreading the virus to others through sexual contact. If their partner's HIV status is unknown, injecting drug users should continue to use latex condoms with spermicide containing nonoxynol-9 to protect themselves from becoming infected.

    Women who are using injectable drugs or having unprotected sex with men who have engaged in high risk behavior are advised that if they are infected and become pregnant, they can pass the virus to their babies. The State Health Department recommends that all women of childbearing age obtain voluntary, HIV antibody testing to determine their health status prior to becoming pregnant.

    b. Safety Protocols: All occupational groups that are involved in tasks which may result in contact with blood and other body fluids (e.g., vaginal secretions, semen, the fluids that surround internal organs) are advised to take special precautions. Safety guidelines have been developed for health care workers, laboratory personnel, public safety workers, ambulance personnel, funeral directors, prison personnel and others.

Because it is not always possible to know who has a blood-borne infection, it is recommended that these precautions be taken at all times:

- Handwashing after contact with any bodily secretions or excretions;
- Uses of protective clothing (gloves, gowns and/or goggles) appropriate to the task being performed, when exposure to blood or body fluids is likely;
- Proper disposal of needles and sharp instruments.

c. Screening of Blood: All blood collected in the U.S. has been tested for HIV antibodies since June 1985. Blood that tests positive is eliminated from the transfusion pool. People with HIV infection and people who have engaged in risk behavior are advised to refrain from donating blood.

d. Screening of Semen, Organs, and Tissues: All potential semen, organ, and tissue donors are tested for antibodies to HIV. In addition, semen donations are quarantined for six months and retested for HIV antibodies prior to release.

e. Anonymous HIV Antibody Testing: Anonymous HIV antibody testing is provided free by New York State for people who wish to determine if they are infected with HIV. At these test sites, it is not necessary to give your name, address, or any identifying information.

f. Confidential HIV Antibody Testing: Confidential HIV antibody testing is also offered free by many local health departments and by state-supported clinics, such as prenatal care and family planning services and community health centers. Many private physicians also provide confidential testing. Test results and medical records are protected by state law from unauthorized disclosure.

84. What services are available to people with HIV, AIDS, or those at risk for the disease?

A network of state-funded programs provide educational and outreach services associated with HIV infection and AIDS. Services include:

- Informational hotlines;
- Education and training sessions;
- Educational materials;
- Free HIV counseling and testing;
- Counseling for patients with HIV or AIDS, their families, and those at risk for HIV infection;
- Support groups;
- Assistance in locating medical, dental, and other health services;
- Transportation to medical care;
- Assistance with insurance coverage, housing, civil rights, and legal issues.

85. Why doesn't the State make everyone take the HIV antibody test?

   Making everyone take the HIV antibody test could be counterproductive. It could scare off those individuals who might benefit most from counseling and testing. This would eliminate the opportunity for counseling regarding HIV prevention, risk reduction and referral for medical treatment. To encourage participation by those at risk, New York State law provides voluntary testing. Under the law, written consent must be given before anyone can be tested for HIV in New York State.

86. What is being done to notify partners of people infected with HIV?

   HIV counselors discuss partner notification techniques with clients who prefer to speak to their partners directly. The State offers a Partner Notification Assistance Program that will help individuals infected with HIV locate and inform their sex and injectable drug-needle sharing partners that they have been exposed to HIV. All information is strictly confidential, and the identity of the person infected with HIV is protected.

87. Why doesn't the government isolate or quarantine people with HIV and AIDS to prevent the spread of the disease?

   People with HIV infection or AIDS do not pose a risk to the public through casual contact. New York State strongly upholds the position that the civil rights of any individual or group should not be abridged by society without scientific evidence that it is necessary. All information accumulated during the past decade indicates that HIV is spread only through direct contact with infected blood, semen, vaginal secretions, or breast milk. It is not spread through the air, food, or casual contact with people who have HIV infection, AIDS, or by objects they have handled or used.

88. What is being done to halt the spread of HIV among IV drug users?

   States have expanded drug addiction programs and are also conducting HIV counseling and testing through a variety of sites serving individuals who may be at risk for HIV infection as a result of drug use.

89. What is being done to get accurate information to the public about HIV and AID?

   The State Health Department maintains toll-free hotlines (1-800-541-AIDS, 1-800-233-SIDA, and 1-800-872-2777) that provide up-to-date information about HIV and AIDS. The State also funds local hotlines and educational activities conducted by regional AIDS task forces and other community groups. TV and radio public service announcement, pamphlets, and brochures directed to the general public and to those who have engaged in behaviors that place them at risk have been developed and are being distributed state-wide. Educational forums are provided for occupational and community groups that have concerns related to HIV and AIDS. AIDS prevention education is required in all schools in the state.

## HUMAN RIGHTS ISSUES

90. What rights do people with HIV infection or AIDS have?

    People with HIV infection or AIDS have the same rights as other citizens in New York State. Unfortunately, some of them have been treated unfairly by employers, landlords, neighbors, co-workers, and others out of unwarranted fear of HIV. Such actions are discriminatory and illegal in New York State. People with HIV infection or AIDS who believe they are being discriminated against may file a complaint with the State Division of Human Rights at 1-800-523-AIDS.

91. What protections are provided by HIV Confidentiality Law?

    This law requires that counseling and written, informed consent take place before an HIV-related test is performed on a person. The law also protects the confidentiality of HIV-related information. People who feel that HIV-related information about them has been released without their consent may file a complaint through the Health Department's Confidentiality Hotline. Unauthorized disclosure of confidential HIV-related information by health or social service workers is subject to civil and/or criminal penalties under the law.

92. Can doctors notify someone that their partner has tested positive for HIV?

    Under the HIV confidentiality law, doctors must counsel a patient with HIV to notify his/her sexual or needle-sharing partners or to seek help in doing so from public health officials. If a patient refuses to do so, the physician may, without the patient's consent, notify a sexual or needle-sharing partner known to be at risk for HIV infection. However, the physician shall not reveal the patient's name to the partner.

93. Can you be fired because you have HIV infection or AIDS?

    No. You cannot be fired solely on the basis of your HIV status. Some employers are reportedly discriminating against persons with HIV infection despite continued advice from public health officials that there is no reason to exclude them from employment as long as they feel well enough to work and can perform their job functions adequately. Those who believe they are being discriminated against by employers may file complaints with the State Division of Human Rights at 1-800-523-AIDS.

94. Should people with HIV infection be banned from working in jobs which involve contact with the public?

    There have been no cases of AIDS that are suspected of having been transmitted through casual contact or through the air, food or water. If a person with HIV infection or AIDS is well enough to work, he/she should be allowed to do so.

95. Can hospital workers or ambulance personnel refuse to care for a person with HIV infection or AIDS?

    Health care workers who refuse to care for a person with HIV infection or AIDS may be subject to firing and possible disciplinary action. Hospitals and ambulance services have a legal responsibility to care for the sick, and to assemble a staff capable of carrying out that mission. There is a need for ongoing education for all health care workers to ensure that they understand the potential routes of HIV transmission and follow recommended safety precautions.

96. Can funeral directors refuse to embalm individuals who have died from AIDS or HIV-related illnesses?

    No. Funeral homes are required by human rights laws not to discriminate against deceased people or their families based solely on the HIV infection or the AIDS diagnosis of the deceased. However, if a funeral director does not embalm in their practice, they cannot be required to embalm individuals who have died from HIV-related illness or AIDS.

**HOW TO REDUCE THE RISK OF HIV INFECTION**

HIV is not an easily transmissible virus. HIV is spread by direct contact with infected body fluids which include blood, semen, vaginal secretions, and breast milk. Direct contact with other infected body fluids containing visible blood also may increase the risk of infection.

Based on this information, the following precautions will not eliminate your risk for HIV infection, but rather reduce your risk of contracting or spreading the virus:

**SAFER SEX**

- Talk to your partner about safer sex. Unless you are certain that your partner is not infected with HIV, you need to protect yourself from HIV and other sexually transmitted diseases (STD's).

- Always use a latex condom when having anal, oral or vaginal sex. (Natural skin or lambskin condoms do not provide an effective barrier against HIV.)

- Use a latex condom with a spermicide containing nonoxynol-9 to further reduce your risk for HIV infection for vaginal and anal sex. (See Question 17.)

- When using a lubricant with a latex condom, always use a water-based lubricant such as K-Y jelly. (Oil-based lubricants such as Vaseline cause latex condoms to break.)

- An unlubricated or dry latex condom should be used for oral sex. For additional protection against HIV, apply a small amount of spermicide containing nonoxynol-9 inside the tip of the condom.

- Use of a diaphragm with a spermicide containing nonoxynol-9 may provide some protection against HIV. However, this method provides far less protection than using a latex condom.

- Use of a spermicide alone may provide some protection against HIV. However, this method of risk reduction should only be used as a <u>very last resort</u>, when the only alternative is unprotected sex.

**INJECTABLE DRUGS**

HIV can be transmitted by sharing needles and works used to inject any substance, such as heroin, cocaine, steroids, etc., into the veins, muscles, or under the skin (skin popping).

- It's best to seek treatment and not use injectable drugs; but if you do inject drugs, don't share needles or works.

- Always clean drug injection equipment with bleach before each use, even if it seems to be packaged as new.

- Clean injection equipment (needles and works) with undiluted bleach and rinse with clean water. Do this by drawing the bleach up through the needle to fill the syringe, shake the set, then squirt it out. Repeat this 2 or 3 times. Follow this by drawing clean water up through the needle into the syringe and squirt it out. Repeat this 2 or 3 times. Never shoot or drink the bleach.

- Do not reuse cotton, water, or cooker. However, if you must reuse the cooker, soak it in bleach and then rinse it with clean water.

- Since bleach loses its effectiveness from exposure to light, store all bleach for cleaning needles and works in an opaque container.

**NON-INJECTABLE DRUGS**

- Using non-injectable, mood-altering drugs can also put you at risk of being infected with HIV. Drugs such as alcohol, marijuana or crack cocaine lower your ability to make good decisions regarding safer sex methods and cleaning needles and works prior to use.

**OTHER PRECAUTIONARY MEASURES**

- Do not share needles for tattooing or piercing any body parts (e.g., ears, nose, etc.).

- Avoid sharing toothbrushes, razors, or other personal items that could have blood on them.

- Health workers, laboratory personnel, funeral home workers, and others whose work may involve contact with body fluids should strictly follow recommended safety procedures to minimize exposure to HIV, hepatitis B, and other blood-borne infections.

- People with HIV infection, AIDS, or those whose behavior has placed them at risk for HIV infection should not donate blood, plasma, body organs, sperm, bone marrow, or other tissue.

- People with HIV infection or AIDS should avoid any sexual activity that could result in direct contact of body fluids. However, if you do participate in sexual activity where direct contact of body fluids could occur, use a latex condom with a spermicide containing nonoxynol-9 to reduce your partner's risk for HIV infection.

- Women with HIV infection or AIDS should understand that if they become pregnant their babies are at increased risk for HIV. Women with HIV infection or AIDS are advised to refrain from nursing their infants, since the virus has been transmitted through breast milk.

- People with HIV infection or AIDS should have regular medical checkups.

# PHILOSOPHY, PRINCIPLES, PRACTICES, AND TECHNICS OF SUPERVISION, ADMINISTRATION, MANAGEMENT, AND ORGANIZATION

## TABLE OF CONTENTS

| | Page |
|---|---|
| MEANING OF SUPERVISION | 1 |
| THE OLD AND THE NEW SUPERVISION | 1 |
| THE EIGHT (8) BASIC PRINCIPLES OF THE NEW SUPERVISION | 1 |
|     I. Principle of Responsibility | 1 |
|     II. Principle of Authority | 2 |
|     III. Principle of Self-Growth | 2 |
|     IV. Principle of Individual Worth | 2 |
|     V. Principle of Creative Leadership | 2 |
|     VI. Principle of Success and Failure | 2 |
|     VII. Principle of Science | 3 |
|     VIII. Principle of Cooperation | 3 |
| WHAT IS ADMINISTRATION? | 3 |
|     I. Practices Commonly Classed as "Supervisory" | 3 |
|     II. Practices Commonly Classed as "Administrative" | 3 |
|     III. Practices Commonly Classed as Both "Supervisory" and "Administrative" | 4 |
| RESPONSIBILITIES OF THE SUPERVISOR | 4 |
| COMPETENCIES OF THE SUPERVISOR | 4 |
| THE PROFESSIONAL SUPERVISOR-EMPLOYEE RELATIONSHIP | 4 |
| MINI-TEXT IN SUPERVISION, ADMINISTRATION, MANAGEMENT, AND ORGANIZATION | 5 |
|     I. Brief Highlights | 5 |
|         A. Levels of Management | 6 |
|         B. What the Supervisor Must Learn | 6 |
|         C. A Definition of Supervision | 6 |
|         D. Elements of the Team Concept | 6 |
|         E. Principles of Organization | 6 |
|         F. The Four Important Parts of Every Job | 7 |
|         G. Principles of Delegation | 7 |
|         H. Principles of Effective Communications | 7 |
|         I. Principles of Work Improvement | 7 |
|         J. Areas of Job Improvement | 7 |
|         K. Seven Key Points in Making Improvements | 8 |

|     |                                              |    |
|-----|----------------------------------------------|----|
| L.  | Corrective Techniques for Job Improvement    | 8  |
| M.  | A Planning Checklist                         | 8  |
| N.  | Five Characteristics of Good Directions      | 9  |
| O.  | Types of Directions                          | 9  |
| P.  | Controls                                     | 9  |
| Q.  | Orienting the New Employee                   | 9  |
| R.  | Checklist for Orienting New Employees        | 9  |
| S.  | Principles of Learning                       | 10 |
| T.  | Causes of Poor Performance                   | 10 |
| U.  | Four Major Steps in On-the-Job Instructions  | 10 |
| V.  | Employees Want Five Things                   | 10 |
| W.  | Some Don'ts in Regard to Praise              | 11 |
| X.  | How to Gain Your Workers' Confidence         | 11 |
| Y.  | Sources of Employee Problems                 | 11 |
| Z.  | The Supervisor's Key to Discipline           | 11 |
| AA. | Five Important Processes of Management       | 12 |
| BB. | When the Supervisor Fails to Plan            | 12 |
| CC. | Fourteen General Principles of Management    | 12 |
| DD. | Change                                       | 12 |

II. Brief Topical Summaries — 13
- A. Who/What is the Supervisor? — 13
- B. The Sociology of Work — 13
- C. Principles and Practices of Supervision — 14
- D. Dynamic Leadership — 14
- E. Processes for Solving Problems — 15
- F. Training for Results — 15
- G. Health, Safety, and Accident Prevention — 16
- H. Equal Employment Opportunity — 16
- I. Improving Communications — 16
- J. Self-Development — 17
- K. Teaching and Training — 17
  1. The Teaching Process — 17
     - a. Preparation — 17
     - b. Presentation — 18
     - c. Summary — 18
     - d. Application — 18
     - e. Evaluation — 18
  2. Teaching Methods — 18
     - a. Lecture — 18
     - b. Discussion — 18
     - c. Demonstration — 19
     - d. Performance — 19
     - e. Which Method to Use — 19

# PHILOSOPHY, PRINCIPLES, PRACTICES, AND TECHNICS
# OF
# SUPERVISION, ADMINISTRATION, MANAGEMENT, AND ORGANIZATION

## MEANING OF SUPERVISION

The extension of the democratic philosophy has been accompanied by an extension in the scope of supervision. Modern leaders and supervisors no longer think of supervision in the narrow sense of being confined chiefly to visiting employees, supplying materials, or rating the staff. They regard supervision as being intimately related to all the concerned agencies of society, they speak of the supervisor's function in terms of "growth," rather than the "improvement" of employees.

This modern concept of supervision may be defined as follows: Supervision is leadership and the development of leadership within groups which are cooperatively engaged in inspection, research, training, guidance, and evaluation.

## THE OLD AND THE NEW SUPERVISION

### TRADITIONAL
1. Inspection
2. Focused on the employee
3. Visitation
4. Random and haphazard
5. Imposed and authoritarian
6. One person usually

### MODERN
1. Study and analysis
2. Focused on aims, materials, methods, supervisors, employees, environment
3. Demonstrations, intervisitation, workshops, directed reading, bulletins, etc.
4. Definitely organized and planned (scientific)
5. Cooperative and democratic
6. Many persons involved (creative)

## THE EIGHT (8) BASIC PRINCIPLES OF THE NEW SUPERVISION

I. Principle of Responsibility
   Authority to act and responsibility for acting must be joined.
   A. If you give responsibility, give authority.
   B. Define employee duties clearly.
   C. Protect employees from criticism by others.
   D. Recognize the rights as well as obligations of employees.
   E. Achieve the aims of a democratic society insofar as it is possible within the area of your work.
   F. Establish a situation favorable to training and learning.
   G. Accept ultimate responsibility for everything done in your section, unit, office, division, department.
   H. Good administration and good supervision are inseparable.

II. Principle of Authority
The success of the supervisor is measured by the extent to which the power of authority is not used.
   A. Exercise simplicity and informality in supervision
   B. Use the simplest machinery of supervision
   C. If it is good for the organization as a whole, it is probably justified.
   D. Seldom be arbitrary or authoritative.
   E. Do not base your work on the power of position or of personality.
   F. Permit and encourage the free expression of opinions.

III. Principle of Self-Growth
The success of the supervisor is measured by the extent to which, and the speed with which, he is no longer needed.
   A. Base criticism on principles, not on specifics.
   B. Point out higher activities to employees.
   C. Train for self-thinking by employees to meet new situations.
   D. Stimulate initiative, self-reliance, and individual responsibility
   E. Concentrate on stimulating the growth of employees rather than on removing defects.

IV. Principle of Individual Worth
Respect for the individual is a paramount consideration in supervision.
   A. Be human and sympathetic in dealing with employees.
   B. Don't nag about things to be done.
   C. Recognize the individual differences among employees and seek opportunities to permit best expression of each personality.

V. Principle of Creative Leadership
The best supervision is that which is not apparent to the employee.
   A. Stimulate, don't drive employees to creative action.
   B. Emphasize doing good things.
   C. Encourage employees to do what they do best.
   D. Do not be too greatly concerned with details of subject or method.
   E. Do not be concerned exclusively with immediate problems and activities.
   F. Reveal higher activities and make them both desired and maximally possible.
   G. Determine procedures in the light of each situation but see that these are derived from a sound basic philosophy.
   H. Aid, inspire, and lead so as to liberate the creative spirit latent in all good employees.

VI. Principle of Success and Failure
There are no unsuccessful employees, only unsuccessful supervisors who have failed to give proper leadership.
   A. Adapt suggestions to the capacities, attitudes, and prejudices of employees.
   B. Be gradual, be progressive, be persistent.
   C. Help the employee find the general principle; have the employee apply his own problem to the general principle.
   D. Give adequate appreciation for good work and honest effort.
   E. Anticipate employee difficulties and help to prevent them.
   F. Encourage employees to do the desirable things they will do anyway.
   G. Judge your supervision by the results it secures.

VII. Principle of Science
Successful supervision is scientific, objective, and experimental. It is based on facts, not on prejudices.
   A. Be cumulative in results.
   B. Never divorce your suggestions from the goals of training.
   C. Don't be impatient of results.
   D. Keep all matters on a professional, not a personal, level.
   E. Do not be concerned exclusively with immediate problems and activities.
   F. Use objective means of determining achievement and rating where possible.

VIII. Principle of Cooperation
Supervision is a cooperative enterprise between supervisor and employee.
   A. Begin with conditions as they are.
   B. Ask opinions of all involved when formulating policies.
   C. Organization is as good as its weakest link.
   D. Let employees help to determine policies and department programs.
   E. Be approachable and accessible—physically and mentally.
   F. Develop pleasant social relationships.

## WHAT IS ADMINISTRATION

Administration is concerned with providing the environment, the material facilities, and the operational procedures that will promote the maximum growth and development of supervisors and employees. (Organization is an aspect and a concomitant of administration.)

There is no sharp line of demarcation between supervision and administration; these functions are intimately interrelated and, often, overlapping. They are complementary activities.

I. Practices Commonly Classed as "Supervisory"
   A. Conducting employees' conferences
   B. Visiting sections, units, offices, divisions, departments
   C. Arranging for demonstrations
   D. Examining plans
   E. Suggesting professional reading
   F. Interpreting bulletins
   G. Recommending in-service training courses
   H. Encouraging experimentation
   I. Appraising employee morale
   J. Providing for intervisitation

II. Practices Commonly Classified as "Administrative"
   A. Management of the office
   B. Arrangement of schedules for extra duties
   C. Assignment of rooms or areas
   D. Distribution of supplies
   E. Keeping records and reports
   F. Care of audio-visual materials
   G. Keeping inventory records
   H. Checking record cards and books

I. Programming special activities
J. Checking on the attendance and punctuality of employees

III. Practices Commonly Classified as Both "Supervisory" and "Administrative"
   A. Program construction
   B. Testing or evaluating outcomes
   C. Personnel accounting
   D. Ordering instructional materials

## RESPONSIBILITIES OF THE SUPERVISOR

A person employed in a supervisory capacity must constantly be able to improve his own efficiency and ability. He represent the employer to the employees and only continuous self-examination can make him a capable supervisor.

Leadership and training are the supervisor's responsibility. An efficient working unit is one in which the employees work with the supervisor. It is his job to bring out the best in his employees. He must always be relaxed, courteous, and calm in his association with his employees. Their feelings are important, and a harsh attitude does not develop the most efficient employees.

## COMPETENCES OF THE SUPERVISOR

I. Complete knowledge of the duties and responsibilities of his position.
II. To be able to organize a job, plan ahead, and carry through.
III. To have self-confidence and initiative.
IV. To be able to handle the unexpected situation and make quick decisions.
V. To be able to properly train subordinates in the positions they are best suited for.
VI. To be able to keep good human relations among his subordinates.
VII. To be able to keep good human relations between his subordinates and himself and to earn their respect and trust.

## THE PROFESSIONAL SUPERVISOR-EMPLOYEE RELATIONSHIP

There are two kinds of efficiency: one kind is only apparent and is produced in organizations through the exercise of mere discipline; this is but a simulation of the second, or true, efficiency which springs from spontaneous cooperation. If you are a manager, no matter how great or small your responsibility, it is your job, in the final analysis, to create and develop this involuntary cooperation among the people whom you supervise. For, no matter how powerful a combination of money, machines, and materials a company may have, this is a dead and sterile thing without a team of willing, thinking, and articulate people to guide it.

The following 21 points are presented as indicative of the exemplary basic relationship that should exist between supervisor and employee:

1. Each person wants to be liked and respected by his fellow employee and wants to be treated with consideration and respect by his superior.
2. The most competent employee will make an error. However, in a unit where good relations exist between the supervisor and his employees, tenseness and fear do not exist. Thus, errors are not hidden or covered up, and the efficiency of a unit is not impaired.

3. Subordinates resent rules, regulations, or orders that are unreasonable or unexplained.
4. Subordinates are quick to resent unfairness, harshness, injustices, and favoritism.
5. An employee will accept responsibility if he knows that he will be complimented for a job well done, and not too harshly chastised for failure; that his supervisor will check the cause of the failure, and, if it was the supervisor's fault, he will assume the blame therefore. If it was the employee's fault, his supervisor will explain the correct method or means of handling the responsibility.
6. An employee wants to receive credit for a suggestion he has made, that is used. If a suggestion cannot be used, the employee is entitled to an explanation. The supervisor should not say "no" and close the subject.
7. Fear and worry slow up a worker's ability. Poor working environment can impair his physical and mental health. A good supervisor avoids forceful methods, threats, and arguments to get a job done.
8. A forceful supervisor is able to train his employees individually and as a team, and is able to motivate them in the proper channels.
9. A mature supervisor is able to properly evaluate his subordinates and to keep them happy and satisfied.
10. A sensitive supervisor will never patronize his subordinates.
11. A worthy supervisor will respect his employees' confidences.
12. Definite and clear-cut responsibilities should be assigned to each executive.
13. Responsibility should always be coupled with corresponding authority.
14. No change should be made in the scope or responsibilities of a position without a definite understanding to that effect on the part of all persons concerned.
15. No executive or employee, occupying a single position in the organization, should be subject to definite orders from more than one source.
16. Orders should never be given to subordinates over the head of a responsible executive. Rather than do this, the officer in question should be supplanted.
17. Criticisms of subordinates should, whoever possible, be made privately, and in no case should a subordinate be criticized in the presence of executives or employees of equal or lower rank.
18. No dispute or difference between executives or employees as to authority or responsibilities should be considered too trivial for prompt and careful adjudication.
19. Promotions, wage changes, and disciplinary action should always be approved by the executive immediately superior to the one directly responsible.
20. No executive or employee should ever be required, or expected, to be at the same time an assistant to, and critic of, another.
21. Any executive whose work is subject to regular inspection should, wherever practicable, be given the assistance and facilities necessary to enable him to maintain an independent check of the quality of his work.

**MINI-TEXT IN SUPERVISION, ADMINISTRATION, MANAGEMENT, AND ORGANIZATION**

I. Brief Highlights

Listed concisely and sequentially are major headings and important data in the field for quick recall and review.

A. Levels of Management
Any organization of some size has several levels of management. In terms of a ladder, the levels are:

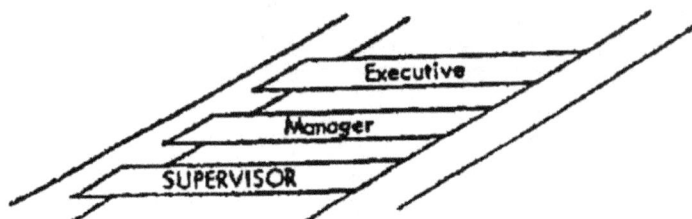

The first level is very important because it is the beginning point of management leadership.

B. What the Supervisor Must Learn
A supervisor must learn to:
1. Deal with people and their differences
2. Get the job done through people
3. Recognize the problems when they exist
4. Overcome obstacles to good performance
5. Evaluate the performance of people
6. Check his own performance in terms of accomplishment

C. A Definition of Supervisor
The term supervisor means any individual having authority, in the interests of the employer, to hire, transfer, suspend, lay-off, recall, promote, discharge, assign, reward, or discipline other employees or responsibility to direct them, or to adjust their grievances, or effectively to recommend such action, if, in connection with the foregoing, exercise of such authority is not of a merely routine or clerical nature but requires the use of independent judgment.

D. Elements of the Team Concept
What is involved in teamwork? The component parts are:
1. Members
2. A leader
3. Goals
4. Plans
5. Cooperation
6. Spirit

E. Principles of Organization
1. A team member must know what his job is.
2. Be sure that the nature and scope of a job are understood.
3. Authority and responsibility should be carefully spelled out.
4. A supervisor should be permitted to make the maximum number of decisions affecting his employees.
5. Employees should report to only one supervisor.
6. A supervisor should direct only as many employees as he can handle effectively.
7. An organization plan should be flexible.

8. Inspection and performance of work should be separate.
9. Organizational problems should receive immediate attention.
10. Assign work in line with ability and experience.

F. The Four Important Parts of Every Job
1. Inherent in every job is the *accountability* for results.
2. A second set of factors in every job is *responsibilities*.
3. Along with duties and responsibilities one must have the *authority* to act within certain limits without obtaining permission to proceed.
4. No job exists in a vacuum. The supervisor is surrounded by key *relationships*.

G. Principles of Delegation
Where work is delegated for the first time, the supervisor should think in terms of these questions:
1. Who is best qualified to do this?
2. Can an employee improve his abilities by doing this?
3. How long should an employee spend on this?
4. Are there any special problems for which he will need guidance?
5. How broad a delegation can I make?

H. Principles of Effective Communications
1. Determine the media.
2. To whom directed?
3. Identification and source authority.
4. Is communication understood?

I. Principles of Work Improvement
1. Most people usually do only the work which is assigned to them.
2. Workers are likely to fit assigned work into the time available to perform it.
3. A good workload usually stimulates output.
4. People usually do their best work when they know that results will be reviewed or inspected.
5. Employees usually feel that someone else is responsible for conditions of work, workplace layout, job methods, type of tools/equipment, and other such factors.
6. Employees are usually defensive about their job security.
7. Employees have natural resistance to change.
8. Employees can support or destroy a supervisor.
9. A supervisor usually earns the respect of his people through his personal example of diligence and efficiency.

J. Areas of Job Improvement
The areas of job improvement are quite numerous, but the most common ones which a supervisor can identify and utilize are:
1. Departmental layout
2. Flow of work
3. Workplace layout
4. Utilization of manpower
5. Work methods
6. Materials handling

7. Utilization
8. Motion economy

K. Seven Key Points in Making Improvements
1. Select the job to be improved
2. Study how it is being done now
3. Question the present method
4. Determine actions to be taken
5. Chart proposed method
6. Get approval and apply
7. Solicit worker participation

L. Corrective Techniques of Job Improvement
Specific Problems
1. Size of workload
2. Inability to meet schedules
3. Strain and fatigue
4. Improper use of men and skills
5. Waste, poor quality, unsafe conditions
6. Bottleneck conditions that hinder output
7. Poor utilization of equipment and machine
8. Efficiency and productivity of labor

General Improvement
1. Departmental layout
2. Flow of work
3. Work plan layout
4. Utilization of manpower
5. Work methods
6. Materials handling
7. Utilization of equipment
8. Motion economy

Corrective Techniques
1. Study with scale model
2. Flow chart study
3. Motion analysis
4. Comparison of units produced to standard allowance
5. Methods analysis
6. Flow chart and equipment study
7. Down time vs. running time
8. Motion analysis

M. A Planning Checklist
1. Objectives
2. Controls
3. Delegations
4. Communications
5. Resources
6. Manpower

7. Equipment
8. Supplies and materials
9. Utilization of time
10. Safety
11. Money
12. Work
13. Timing of improvements

N. Five Characteristics of Good Directions
In order to get results, directions must be:
1. Possible of accomplishment
2. Agreeable with worker interests
3. Related to mission
4. Planned and complete
5. Unmistakably clear

O. Types of Directions
1. Demands or direct orders
2. Requests
3. Suggestion or implication
4. volunteering

P. Controls
A typical listing of the overall areas in which the supervisor should establish controls might be:
1. Manpower
2. Materials
3. Quality of work
4. Quantity of work
5. Time
6. Space
7. Money
8. Methods

Q. Orienting the New Employee
1. Prepare for him
2. Welcome the new employee
3. Orientation for the job
4. Follow-up

R. Checklist for Orienting New Employees          Yes   No
1. Do you appreciate the feelings of new employees when they first report for work?     ___   ___
2. Are you aware of the fact that the new employee must make a big adjustment to his job?     ___   ___
3. Have you given him good reasons for liking the job and the organization?     ___   ___
4. Have you prepared for his first day on the job?     ___   ___
5. Did you welcome him cordially and make him feel needed?     ___   ___

|   |   | Yes | No |
|---|---|---|---|

6. Did you establish rapport with him so that he feels free to talk and discuss matters with you? ____ ____
7. Did you explain his job to him and his relationship to you? ____ ____
8. Does he know that his work will be evaluated periodically on a basis that is fair and objective? ____ ____
9. Did you introduce him to his fellow workers in such a way that they are likely to accept him? ____ ____
10. Does he know what employee benefits he will receive? ____ ____
11. Does he understand the importance of being on the job and what to do if he must leave his duty station? ____ ____
12. Has he been impressed with the importance of accident prevention and safe practice? ____ ____
13. Does he generally know his way around the department? ____ ____
14. Is he under the guidance of a sponsor who will teach the right way of doing things? ____ ____
15. Do you plan to follow-up so that he will continue to adjust successfully to his job? ____ ____

S. Principles of Learning
   1. Motivation
   2. Demonstration or explanation
   3. Practice

T. Causes of Poor Performance
   1. Improper training for job
   2. Wrong tools
   3. Inadequate directions
   4. Lack of supervisory follow-up
   5. Poor communications
   6. Lack of standards of performance
   7. Wrong work habits
   8. Low morale
   9. Other

U. Four Major Steps in On-The-Job Instruction
   1. Prepare the worker
   2. Present the operation
   3. Tryout performance
   4. Follow-up

V. Employees Want Five Things
   1. Security
   2. Opportunity
   3. Recognition
   4. Inclusion
   5. Expression

W. Some Don'ts in Regard to Praise
1. Don't praise a person for something he hasn't done.
2. Don't praise a person unless you can be sincere.
3. Don't be sparing in praise just because your superior withholds it from you.
4. Don't let too much time elapse between good performance and recognition of it

X. How to Gain Your Workers' Confidence
Methods of developing confidence include such things as:
1. Knowing the interests, habits, hobbies of employees
2. Admitting your own inadequacies
3. Sharing and telling of confidence in others
4. Supporting people when they are in trouble
5. Delegating matters that can be well handled
6. Being frank and straightforward about problems and working conditions
7. Encouraging others to bring their problems to you
8. Taking action on problems which impede worker progress

Y. Sources of Employee Problems
On-the-job causes might be such things as:
1. A feeling that favoritism is exercised in assignments
2. Assignment of overtime
3. An undue amount of supervision
4. Changing methods or systems
5. Stealing of ideas or trade secrets
6. Lack of interest in job
7. Threat of reduction in force
8. Ignorance or lack of communications
9. Poor equipment
10. Lack of knowing how supervisor feels toward employee
11. Shift assignments

Off-the-job problems might have to do with:
1. Health
2. Finances
3. Housing
4. Family

Z. The Supervisor's Key to Discipline
There are several key points about discipline which the supervisor should keep in mind:
1. Job discipline is one of the disciplines of life and is directed by the supervisor.
2. It is more important to correct an employee fault than to fix blame for it.
3. Employee performance is affected by problems both on the job and off.
4. Sudden or abrupt changes in behavior can be indications of important employee problems.
5. Problems should be dealt with as soon as possible after they are identified.
6. The attitude of the supervisor may have more to do with solving problems than the techniques of problem solving.
7. Correction of employee behavior should be resorted to only after the supervisor is sure that training or counseling will not be helpful.

8. Be sure to document your disciplinary actions.
9. Make sure that you are disciplining on the basis of facts rather than personal feelings.
10. Take each disciplinary step in order, being careful not to make snap judgments, or decisions based on impatience.

AA. Five Important Processes of Management
1. Planning
2. Organizing
3. Scheduling
4. Controlling
5. Motivating

BB. When the Supervisor Fails to Plan
1. Supervisor creates impression of not knowing his job
2. May lead to excessive overtime
3. Job runs itself—supervisor lacks control
4. Deadlines and appointments missed
5. Parts of the work go undone
6. Work interrupted by emergencies
7. Sets a bad example
8. Uneven workload creates peaks and valleys
9. Too much time on minor details at expense of more important tasks

CC. Fourteen General Principles of Management
1. Division of work
2. Authority and responsibility
3. Discipline
4. Unity of command
5. Unity of direction
6. Subordination of individual interest to general interest
7. Remuneration of personnel
8. Centralization
9. Scalar chain
10. Order
11. Equity
12. Stability of tenure of personnel
13. Initiative
14. Esprit de corps

DD. Change

Bringing about change is perhaps attempted more often, and yet less well understood, than anything else the supervisor does. How do people generally react to change? (People tend to resist change that is imposed upon them by other individuals or circumstances.

Change is characteristic of every situation. It is a part of every real endeavor where the efforts of people are concerned.

13

1. Why do people resist change?
   People may resist change because of:
   a. Fear of the unknown
   b. Implied criticism
   c. Unpleasant experiences in the past
   d. Fear of loss of status
   e. Threat to the ego
   f. Fear of loss of economic stability

2. How can we best overcome the resistance to change?
   In initiating change, take these steps:
   a. Get ready to sell
   b. Identify sources of help
   c. Anticipate objections
   d. Sell benefits
   e. Listen in depth
   f. Follow up

II. Brief Topical Summaries

   A. Who/What is the Supervisor?
      1. The supervisor is often called the "highest level employee and the lowest level manager."
      2. A supervisor is a member of both management and the work group. He acts as a bridge between the two.
      3. Most problems in supervision are in the area of human relations, or people problems.
      4. Employees expect: Respect, opportunity to learn and to advance, and a sense of belonging, and so forth.
      5. Supervisors are responsible for directing people and organizing work. Planning is of paramount importance.
      6. A position description is a set of duties and responsibilities inherent to a given position.
      7. It is important to keep the position description up-to-date and to provide each employee with his own copy.

   B. The Sociology of Work
      1. People are alike in many ways; however, each individual is unique.
      2. The supervisor is challenged in getting to know employee differences. Acquiring skills in evaluating individuals is an asset.
      3. Maintaining meaningful working relationships in the organization is of great importance.
      4. The supervisor has an obligation to help individuals to develop to their fullest potential.
      5. Job rotation on a planned basis helps to build versatility and to maintain interest and enthusiasm in work groups.
      6. Cross training (job rotation) provides backup skills.

7. The supervisor can help reduce tension by maintaining a sense of humor, providing guidance to employees, and by making reasonable and timely decisions. Employees respond favorably to working under reasonably predictable circumstances.
8. Change is characteristic of all managerial behavior. The supervisor must adjust to changes in procedures, new methods, technological changes, and to a number of new and sometimes challenging situations.
9. To overcome the natural tendency for people to resist change, the supervisor should become more skillful in initiating change.

C. Principles and Practices of Supervision
1. Employees should be required to answer to only one superior.
2. A supervisor can effectively direct only a limited number of employees, depending upon the complexity, variety, and proximity of the jobs involved.
3. The organizational chart presents the organization in graphic form. It reflects lines of authority and responsibility as well as interrelationships of units within the organization.
4. Distribution of work can be improved through an analysis using the "Work Distribution Chart."
5. The "Work Distribution Chart" reflects the division of work within a unit in understandable form.
6. When related tasks are given to an employee, he has a better chance of increasing his skills through training.
7. The individual who is given the responsibility for tasks must also be given the appropriate authority to insure adequate results.
8. The supervisor should delegate repetitive, routine work. Preparation of recurring reports, maintaining leave and attendance records are some examples.
9. Good discipline is essential to good task performance. Discipline is reflected in the actions of employees on the job in the absence of supervision.
10. Disciplinary action may have to be taken when the positive aspects of discipline have failed. Reprimand, warning, and suspension are examples of disciplinary action.
11. If a situation calls for a reprimand, be sure it is deserved and remember it is to be done in private.

D. Dynamic Leadership
1. A style is a personal method or manner of exerting influence.
2. Authoritarian leaders often see themselves as the source of power and authority.
3. The democratic leader often perceives the group as the source of authority and power.
4. Supervisors tend to do better when using the pattern of leadership that is most natural for them.
5. Social scientists suggest that the effective supervisor use the leadership style that best fits the problem or circumstances involved.
6. All four styles—telling, selling, consulting, joining—have their place. Using one does not preclude using the other at another time.

7. The theory X point of view assumes that the average person dislikes work, will avoid it whenever possible, and must be coerced to achieve organizational objectives.
8. The theory Y point of view assumes that the average person considers work to be a natural as play, and, when the individual is committed, he requires little supervision or direction to accomplish desired objectives.
9. The leader's basic assumptions concerning human behavior and human nature affect his actions, decisions, and other managerial practices.
10. Dissatisfaction among employees is often present, but difficult to isolate. The supervisor should seek to weaken dissatisfaction by keeping promises, being sincere and considerate, keeping employees informed, and so forth.
11. Constructive suggestions should be encouraged during the natural progress of the work.

E. Processes for Solving Problems
1. People find their daily tasks more meaningful and satisfying when they can improve them.
2. The causes of problems, or the key factors, are often hidden in the background. Ability to solve problems often involves the ability to isolate them from their backgrounds. There is some substance to the cliché that some persons "can't see the forest for the trees."
3. New procedures are often developed from old ones. Problems should be broken down into manageable parts. New ideas can be adapted from old one.
4. People think differently in problem-solving situations. Using a logical, patterned approach is often useful. One approach found to be useful includes these steps:
   a. Define the problem
   b. Establish objectives
   c. Get the facts
   d. Weigh and decide
   e. Take action
   f. Evaluate action

F. Training for Results
1. Participants respond best when they feel training is important to them.
2. The supervisor has responsibility for the training and development of those who report to him.
3. When training is delegated to others, great care must be exercised to insure the trainer has knowledge, aptitude, and interest for his work as a trainer.
4. Training (learning) of some type goes on continually. The most successful supervisor makes certain the learning contributes in a productive manner to operational goals.
5. New employees are particularly susceptible to training. Older employees facing new job situations require specific training, as well as having need for development and growth opportunities.
6. Training needs require continuous monitoring.
7. The training officer of an agency is a professional with a responsibility to assist supervisors in solving training problems.

8. Many of the self-development steps important to the supervisor's own growth are equally important to the development of peers and subordinates. Knowledge of these is important when the supervisor consults with others on development and growth opportunities.

G. Health, Safety, and Accident Prevention
1. Management-minded supervisors take appropriate measures to assist employees in maintaining health and in assuring safe practices in the work environment.
2. Effective safety training and practices help to avoid injury and accidents.
3. Safety should be a management goal. All infractions of safety which are observed should be corrected without exception.
4. Employees' safety attitude, training and instruction, provision of safe tools and equipment, supervision, and leadership are considered highly important factors which contribute to safety and which can be influenced directly by supervisors.
5. When accidents do occur, they should be investigated promptly for very important reasons, including the fact that information which is gained can be used to prevent accidents in the future.

H. Equal Employment Opportunity
1. The supervisor should endeavor to treat all employees fairly, without regard to religion, race, sex, or national origin.
2. Groups tend to reflect the attitude of the leader. Prejudice can be detected even in very subtle form. Supervisors must strive to create a feeling of mutual respect and confidence in every employee.
3. Complete utilization of all human resources is a national goal. Equitable consideration should be accorded women in the work force, minority-group members, the physically and mentally handicapped, and the older employee. The important question is: "Who can do the job?"
4. Training opportunities, recognition for performance, overtime assignments, promotional opportunities, and all other personnel actions are to be handled on an equitable basis.

I. Improving Communications
1. Communications is achieving understanding between the sender and the receiver of a message. It also means sharing information—the creation of understanding.
2. Communication is basic to all human activity. Words are means of conveying meanings; however, real meanings are in people.
3. There are very practical differences in the effectiveness of one-way, impersonal, and two-way communications. Words spoken face-to-face are better understood. Telephone conversations are effective, but lack the rapport of person-to-person exchanges. The whole person communicates.
4. Cooperation and communication in an organization go hand in hand. When there is a mutual respect between people, spelling out rules and procedures for communicating is unnecessary.
5. There are several barriers to effective communications. These include failure to listen with respect and understanding, lack of skill in feedback, and misinterpreting the meanings of words used by the speaker. It is also common

practice to listen to what we want to hear, and tune out things we do not want to hear.
6. Communication is management's chief problem. The supervisor should accept the challenge to communicate more effectively and to improve interagency and intra-agency communications.
7. The supervisor may often plan for and conduct meetings. The planning phase is critical and may determine the success or the failure of a meeting.
8. Speaking before groups usually requires extra effort. Stage fright may never disappear completely, but it can be controlled.

J. Self-Development
1. Every employee is responsible for his own self-development.
2. Toastmaster and toastmistress clubs offer opportunities to improve skills in oral communications.
3. Planning for one's own self-development is of vital importance. Supervisors know their own strengths and limitations better than anyone else.
4. Many opportunities are open to aid the supervisor in his developmental efforts, including job assignments; training opportunities, both governmental and non-governmental—to include universities and professional conferences and seminars.
5. Programmed instruction offers a means of studying at one's own rate.
6. Where difficulties may arise from a supervisor's being away from his work for training, he may participate in televised home study or correspondence courses to meet his self-development needs.

K. Teaching and Training
1. The Teaching Process
Teaching is encouraging and guiding the learning activities of students toward established goals. In most cases this process consists of five steps: preparation, presentation, summarization, evaluation, and application.

   a. Preparation
   Preparation is two-fold in nature; that of the supervisor and the employee. Preparation by the supervisor is absolutely essential to success. He must know what, when, where, how, and whom he will teach. Some of the factors that should be considered are:
   1) The objectives
   2) The materials needed
   3) The methods to be used
   4) Employee participation
   5) Employee interest
   6) Training aids
   7) Evaluation
   8) Summarization

   Employee preparation consists in preparing the employee to receive the material. Probably the most important single factor in the preparation of the employee is arousing and maintaining his interest. He must know the objectives of the training, why he is there, how the material can be used, and its importance to him.

b. Presentation
In presentation, have a carefully designed plan and follow it. The plan should be accurate and complete, yet flexible enough to meet situations as they arise. The method of presentation will be determined by the particular situation and objectives.

c. Summary
A summary should be made at the end of every training unit and program. In addition, there may be internal summaries depending on the nature of the material being taught. The important thing is that the trainee must always be able to understand how each part of the new material relates to the whole.

d. Application
The supervisor must arrange work so the employee will be given a chance to apply new knowledge or skills while the material is still clear in his mind and interest is high. The trainee does not really know whether he has learned the material until he has been given a chance to apply it. If the material is not applied, it loses most of its value.

e. Evaluation
The purpose of all training is to promote learning. To determine whether the training has been a success or failure, the supervisor must evaluate this learning.
In the broadest sense, evaluation includes all the devices, methods, skills, and techniques used by the supervisor to keep himself and the employees informed as to their progress toward the objectives they are pursuing. The extent to which the employee has mastered the knowledge, skills, and abilities, or changed his attitudes, as determined by the program objectives, is the extent to which instruction has succeeded or failed.
Evaluation should not be confined to the end of the lesson, day, or program but should be used continuously. We shall note later the way this relates to the rest of the teaching process.

2. Teaching Methods
A teaching method is a pattern of identifiable student and instructor activity used in presenting training material.
All supervisors are faced with the problem of deciding which method should be used at a given time.

a. Lecture
The lecture is direct oral presentation of material by the supervisor. The present trend is to place less emphasis on the trainer's activity and more on that of the trainee.

b. Discussion
Teaching by discussion or conference involves using questions and other techniques to arouse interest and focus attention upon certain areas, and by doing so creating a learning situation. This can be one of the most

valuable methods because it gives the employees an opportunity to express their ideas and pool their knowledge.

c. Demonstration
The demonstration is used to teach how something works or how to do something. It can be used to show a principle or what the results of a series of actions will be. A well-staged demonstration is particularly effective because it shows proper methods of performance in a realistic manner.

d. Performance
Performance is one of the most fundamental of all learning techniques or teaching methods. The trainee may be able to tell how a specific operation should be performed but he cannot be sure he knows how to perform the operation until he has done so.
As with all methods, there are certain advantages and disadvantages to each method.

e. Which Method to Use
Moreover, there are other methods and techniques of teaching. It is difficult to use any method without other methods entering into it. In any learning situation, a combination of methods is usually more effective than any one method alone.

Finally, evaluation must be integrated into the other aspects of the teaching-learning process.

It must be used in the motivation of the trainees; it must be used to assist in developing understanding during the training; and it must be related to employee application of the results of training.

This is distinctly the role of the supervisor.